I don't know your name.
    I don't know when you were born.

I don't know your occupation,
    I don't know where you live.

So am I qualified
    to tell you about yourself?

I'll try, because I am
    no different than you,
    and perhaps you have
    the same aspiration that I do:

    to be fulfilled; to be in peace;
    to experience the ultimate
    expression of life, called joy.

— Prem Rawat

NO ORDINARY BOX

PREM RAWAT

Have You Looked Inside?

20 Talks from Around the World

an **ADI** book

For information, address Words of Peace Global, P.O. Box 2745, CS Amsterdam, The Netherlands.

ISBN: 978-1493764648

Prem Rawat delivers his message of peace to diverse audiences around the world. This compilation, No ORDINARY Box, was derived from his talks and edited for brevity and ease of reading.

ADI means *ancient*: being old in wisdom and experience; dating from a remote period; of great age; having the qualities associated with age, wisdom, or long use; venerable.

No ORDINARY Box can be ordered online at
Amazon
store.wopg.org

Contents

Introduction

Prem Rawat is an international speaker on the topic of personal peace, attracting audiences of all kinds. His life's goal is to offer his message of peace to all seven billion of the world's population.

No Ordinary Box is not a book written by Prem Rawat; it's a compilation of edited talks. These talks have been delivered to a wide range of live audiences, usually lasting about an hour—without a script or prepared notes. The words are truly living words, spoken from his heart during face-to-face interactions with countless people.

What Prem Rawat does in these situations could be described this way: He is a painter. He paints with his words, and he always paints landscapes. They are all landscapes of human existence.

That would make reading this book similar to visiting an exhibition at an art gallery, where you can go around and spend time with each of the 20 large and complex paintings at your own leisure, in the order that you choose.

All the paintings have a myriad of real life scenes in them, but you would soon notice that some elements can be found in each one. There is birth, life, and death. There is the power that created the landscape of existence, and is present as the giver of life. And there is the individual who exists for a limited time, and has a deeply felt desire to make sense of the whole of human existence. And underneath these pictures of the individual, ever surrounded by dilemmas, hardships, ideas, and ambitions, there always lie some fundamental questions: Who am I? Why am I here?

Each of the 20 chapters in this book represents a slightly different perspective of this landscape of human existence. No matter what the perspective may be, the search for fulfillment is in it. To Prem Rawat, these two areas of questioning: Who am I? and How can I be fulfilled?—are part of the same quest. In his words, true joy, happiness and inner peace can only come from knowing who you are, and will come when a person truly knows themselves. And the comedy of the world you see portrayed in all his paintings can be traced back to people simply not being clear about why they are alive. Great timeless stuff!

While selecting the talks for this book (out of many hundreds from recent years) and preparing them for print, it's been striking to me how bold his position is: Know who you are—and your world will profoundly change for the better. And then he adds, "But don't believe me, find out for yourself."

– Ole Grünbaum, Editor

I talk about peace.

It's not about the world.
It's about the individuals.
It's about every single human being.

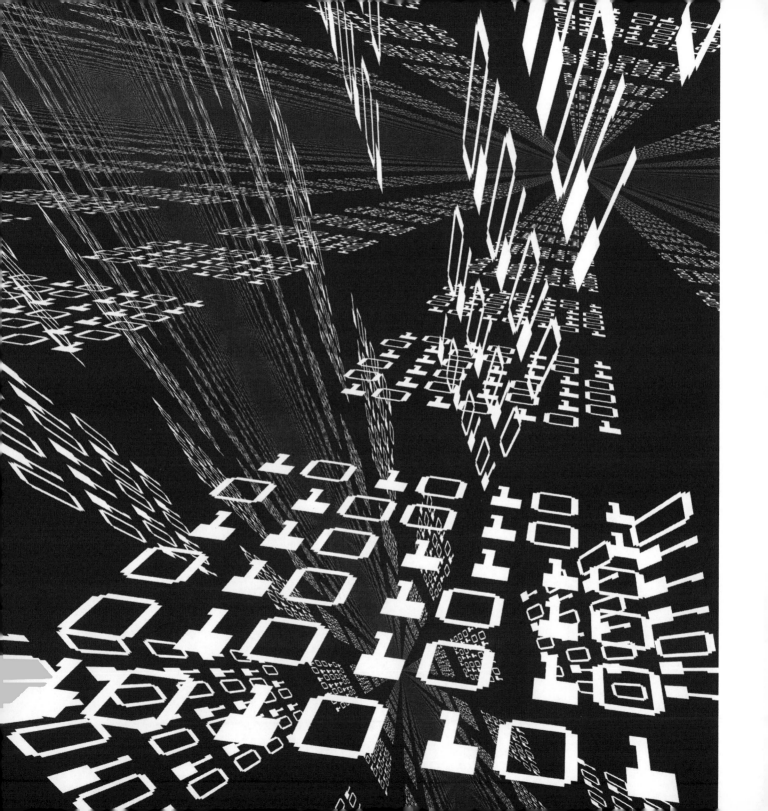

PART ONE

THE QUEST

Why are you alive?

You'll never know
the answer in words,
but you can feel it.

THE QUESTIONS

WHO AM I? WHY AM I HERE?
WHERE DID I COME FROM? WHERE AM I GOING?

For a very, very long time, human beings have asked certain questions. They've looked around themselves and asked, "Where did I come from?" And when they saw people pass away: "Where am I going to?" And, in between: "Why am I here?"

There are many kinds of questions, like "Is there a God?" "What was I in my last lifetime?" or "How long will I live?" But the questions that I am talking about are questions that are valid for every human being. And even today, with so many books, interpretations, religions, and ideas, these questions still remain: "Where did I come from?" "Where am I going to?" "Why am I here?" And ultimately, "Who am I?"

Throughout the eras of history, these questions have sparked different emotions, thoughts, and ideas. Some people are mostly interested in the first two questions: "Where did I come from?" and "Where am I going to go?" Other people are much more attracted by "Why am I here?" and "Who am I?"

In your life, you have to focus on which of these four questions you really want answered. On the subject of "Where did I come from?" and "Where am I going to go?" there is an immense amount of speculation and, somehow, because of the way it is, speculating is all you can do. You can't verify the answers.

However, the other two questions: "Why am I here?" and "Who am I?" require a tremendous amount of consciousness and clarity.

GLOWING DIRT
Sometimes we forget the power of life—the call for living, the call of existence. We forget what it means to be alive. We forget that life is a celebration. We forget that what we want is here, now. We forget how blessed we are that we exist.

Eventually, everybody has to leave. That's the wheel of existence. This is certain. It is going to

14

happen. And there are no formulas. Statistically, it is the young who will see their parents pass away, but sometimes the reverse happens. Parents see the young ones leave. And whoever it is who passes away, there will be sorrow. When someone you love is not here anymore, sorrow comes.

Hopefully, after you have felt the sorrow, you will gather your strength and move on, recognizing what it means to be alive. And in so doing, you will celebrate all life that has ever danced on the face of this earth.

Sometimes as you look up at night, you see the Milky Way and all the stars, and you feel very insignificant. We're not even in the downtown of the galaxy. We're tucked away in a very quiet little corner. And I guess that's a good thing. From where we are, we look around, and we want to know, to see, to understand. I've seen the pictures on different websites of all the celestial bodies out there, and it's amazing. They look incredible, outrageous, yet all they are is dirt.

When people are developing robot cars to use for exploration on the moon or Mars, sometimes they take them to the most desolate places on Earth to see if the cars can survive there. If a car can go up and down on that terrain, then it should have no problem up there, because it's all just dirt— glowing dirt and not-so-glowing dirt—but just dirt and more dirt. And how magnificent the dirt has been made!

Now I say *dirt*, and I say *magnificent*, but the magnificence is not in the dirt. The magnificence is in you. So who are you? Who am I? Well, I am part of that dirt. This is where I came from, and this is where I will go—to dirt. So you might ask, "Is that bad or good? Right or wrong? And why or why not?" But stop for a second. This "human dirt" has magnificence in it. This dirt has the capacity to experience joy, to experience peace. And that is no ordinary feat.

However insignificant you may think or feel you are, you cannot forget the miracle that takes place when the breath comes and the breath goes.

Recognizing what it means to be alive, you will celebrate all life that has ever danced on the face of this earth.

THE POWER OF LIGHT
Understanding the miracle of life should be your passion. Adoring this existence should be your first love. Giving thanks in return should be your duty. And letting nothing come in between you and this appreciation should be your war. If you're going to fight, then fight unconsciousness so that it does not win in your life. Right now you fight, but you fight the wrong wars.

Fight the war you can win. It has nothing to do with your age. It has nothing to do with your physical strength, your intelligence, your cunning, or your education. Fight so that nothing comes between you and this adoration, this love, this joy. Nothing. Then you will have a life that is clear.

The power of light is immense. It is far greater than the power of darkness. A little tiny light can remove a tremendous amount of darkness. You can imagine a captain sailing his ship on a dark night hundreds of years ago. He knows that he could run into rocks and destroy himself, his crew, his cargo, and his ship, all at once. It wouldn't take much. Those ships didn't have reverse engines. They ran on wind power, and whatever wind brought them to the rocks would be sure to pound them until nothing was left.

Sailors would search and search for this little light. It would be very faint as it came across the horizon, but it would be their savior. As soon as they saw the light, they knew where they were, how they had to steer, what they had to avoid. Because of that little light, everything would become apparent. Such is the power of light.

SELF-KNOWLEDGE

People sincerely want to know "Who am I?" and "Why am I here?" I will tie the answers to these questions to the most beautiful word—two words actually, and beautiful when put together: self-knowledge.

Do you think knowledge of the self would answer both of these questions? Here's a little

clue. Trying to answer "Why am I here?" won't necessarily help you find out who you are. But if you can first answer "Who am I?" it'll be a lot easier to figure out the answer to "Why am I here?"

I am part of that dirt.

This is where I came from, and this is where I will go: to dirt.

TURMOIL AND DREAMS

Some people are constantly caught up in their ideas and their turmoil: "Oh, my life! What's going to happen?" How many of those who are in turmoil are actually listening to their own voice? Even those desperate things that you say to yourself aren't in your voice. They're in someone else's voice. And you listen to it: "You good-for-nothing!" "What's going to happen tomorrow?" But what does *your* voice say? Your voice comes from a feeling of just wanting to be content, to be simple, to live, to thrive, to be happy, to be in peace. No more than that. That's your real dream.

The day you figure out who you are, you'll say, "I had it in my pocket all the time."

So many people are searching. They don't know why they are searching, and they don't know what they are searching for. They just search. You ask them what they are doing, and they say, "I'm searching for the truth."

If only you understood who you are, you would know that truth resides in you. You are the container in which truth resides. People say, "I have been searching for God." Why? You search for God, for truth, for this, for that, because you don't know who you are. The day you figure out who you are, you'll say, "I had it in my pocket all the time."

You may think your dream is the one you see in a magazine or a newspaper: "I want this." "I want that." "I want to be like this." "I wish I were like that." "How can I be like this, like that?"

People spend huge amounts of money to look young. The young ones don't care. Even when little girls try on lipstick, they only want to emulate their mom. They don't need lipstick; they don't need eye makeup. They're young. But what is youth anyway? What is this "look" thing?

As you go forward in this march of life, a mask comes off. And as you go on a little more, another mask comes off, a little more, and another one comes off, and another one comes off.

THE INFINITE

These masks keep coming off. Up till what point? Till dirt becomes dirt. Then this process stops. There's no more to evolve. And this connects to the other two questions: "Where did I come from?" and "Where am I going?" You are a combination of two things: the human body and the infinite. You don't deal with the infinite every day; you deal with your body every day. This is what you shave; this is what you have a haircut for; this is what you look at in the mirror. But you are not your body. One more element is involved, and that is the infinite that resides in you. That is what makes you *you!* What is death? It's a simple disconnect of the two.

So the answer depends on what you recognize. If you recognize only the body, the answers to the two questions are: You came from dirt, and you're going to go back to dirt. It's not glamorous, but it's true. If you happen to be so fortunate that you recognize the infinite within you, I have good news for you, because the answer is, you came from the infinite, and you are going to go back to the infinite.

And more than that, while you are here, you can meet, you can get to know, the beautiful that is inside of you. And the joy that springs forth when you do is immeasurable.

MAKE IT HAPPEN

I think I have covered the four questions. The rest is up to you. Think about it. I don't see anyone who does not have the potential to recognize and understand who they are. Regardless of their background, their age, and all those things, this is possible. My advice to you is: Make it happen.

I don't see anyone who does not have the potential to recognize and understand who they are.

TODAY
WAS MADE FOR
YOU

WE HAVE GOTTEN USED TO THE GREATEST LIE THERE IS. IT IS CALLED TOMORROW.

There are people who live by paper mills where the stench is horrible, but after a while they get used to it. They don't smell the stench anymore. So I have to ask myself the question: What have I gotten used to in my life?

Does being confused bother me anymore? It should. Not having clarity in one's life should be very bothersome. Not having understanding in one's life should be painful. Indeed, not knowing one's own self should be intolerable. And where can you go to get away from yourself?

On weekends, people take a trip to the countryside to get away from the city. But when a person doesn't know his or her own self, there is nowhere to go. You are everywhere you go. And you don't know who this person is! How do you tolerate that? You tolerate it by becoming used to it.

19

Is there confusion in the world? Absolutely. There is not one single area in this world where there isn't confusion. And not just a little bit—massive confusion.

How do you live in a world like that? Very easy. You just get used to it. After picking up one newspaper after another; reading about this calamity and that calamity, you get used to it. Are there hungry people in the world? Of course there are. Is that going to stop you from having breakfast tomorrow morning? Absolutely not. Why not? You're used to it.

REALITY

I want to tell you that you should not get used to confusion. Because there is a place inside you that is so magnificent, that is so clear. That is full of understanding, full of answers—not questions. And I'm not just telling you this. I can also make it possible for you to experience it for yourself. To experience the joy that is inside you.

Why is it important for you to experience it and not just hear about it? You have heard about tranquility. You have heard about serenity. You have heard about peace. And somebody could say, "Just keep thinking: Serenity, serenity. Tranquility, tranquility. Peace, peace, peace. Doesn't that feel good?" No, it doesn't. Because tranquility, serenity, and peace need to be felt—not talked or thought about.

Imagine you buy a car, and you go to pick it up and the dealer says, "You now own this car, but you cannot drive it, you cannot take it home. You cannot see it again. You cannot touch it again. But it's yours." That would be silly.

But there are so many things that are like that in our lives. We know about them, but we have gotten used to their absence. We know about God, but we have gotten used to not ever feeling, not ever understanding what God is. And we say, "Okay. Maybe after I die." Why would you leave the most important thing in your life till after you die? Is anybody waiting to die before they can fall in love? Before they can get a vacation? Before they can make some money? Of course not.

TODAY!

That's not living in reality. And it's certainly not living in actuality, either. Because our fervor is always for "now": "I need that big house now." "I need that big car now." "I need that better job now." "I want to be happy now." "I want to be successful now."

You should be in peace *now*. You should have the clarity in your life now. You should have the happiness now. A troubled mind is not good at all. Your heart should be fulfilled now. And what do you think will fulfill your heart? You *know* it. But you have gotten used to ignoring it.

Not knowing one's own self should be intolerable.

And where can you go to get away from yourself?

20

Your heart is fulfilled when it has peace, when it has clarity. Here. Today. Do you know you've been waiting for *today* for a very long time? Every birthday that you had, somebody said to you, "Happy birthday, and may you live a long time." Today was always included in your aspirations.

We have gotten used to the greatest lie there is. It is called *tomorrow*. Why is tomorrow the greatest lie? Because you cannot exist in tomorrow. Tomorrow never comes. Only today comes. So what did you do today?

Do you know how to work on being fulfilled? Did you work on that today? Or did you merely cope? Have you gotten used to coping every day?

Do you like to discuss things? There are people who just love it. I've known about them since I was very young. I was only 13 when I started traveling worldwide. And people would come to me wanting to debate everything.

WORLD WIDE WEB

I am not a debating person. Because there are only two possibilities: Do you know or *don't* you know? If you don't know, don't move your lips. And if you do know, you don't need to move them a whole lot. Just moving your lips doesn't mean anything. Because after a lot of this movement of the lips, at the end of the day, you find yourself still scratching your head.

There are more educated people on the face of this earth than there ever have been. There are more schools now than there ever were. And there is the World Wide Web. What a name! The Internet was first conceived to share information and make information available to the world. So here we are. We have more information at our fingertips than we know what to do with. So what do we do with all that information? We drive ourselves crazy.

If, once in a while, you find you have time to read a book, to laugh, to walk on the beach and enjoy the scenery—if you find yourself having those times, buy a computer, and those times will be gone. Next thing you know, a person who you don't even *know* is sending you email.

Sixty years ago that would have been impossible. Today, your mailbox is full of mail—not from people you know, from people you don't know. They just know your email address. And they're telling you all these things, and selling you things, and being your "friend". And then you hear, "You could open the wrong email and your computer will be destroyed." Do you love fear? If you find you don't have much fear in your life, buy a computer. You will be afraid for the rest of your life. Viruses—absolutely amazing.

The way people play with our heads. Have you seen it on television? Ten minutes ago, "Buy this cake." "Buy this ice cream." "Potato chips." "French fries." Five minutes ago: "Summer is coming, you must fit in your pants. Use this machine, it'll make you lose weight." And I don't know who pays who. Whether the exercise machine people actually pay these other people— Because if you are already fit, and you don't eat all that stuff, you don't need the machine.

We are in a vicious spiral, and everybody is spiraling in it. And people are getting killed around the world. Even with all the education and all the information, innocent people are dying every single day.

YOUR BIRTHRIGHT

How can that be with all the knowledge in the world? Very simple. If self-knowledge is missing, there is bound to be chaos.

There is a place where there is no chaos. That place is inside you. There is a possibility that you can be fulfilled. So you should *not* get used to confusion. You should not get used to doubt. You should not get used to ambiguity. You should not get used to chaos. Being human, you have a birthright—a fundamental right to be fulfilled. Use this right, because what you're looking for is within you. Always has been and always will be.

There is a place where there is no chaos. That place is inside you.

We need to feel. We need to understand. We need to love. We need to love the most lovable, and that most lovable is within us. We need, every day, to feel fulfilled. Excuse me, this is not a luxury. This is a necessity.

A lot of people give lectures. They tell you to smile. They tell you how, with your body language, you can show other people you are happy. It's garbage. Because if you are happy, you don't have to pretend with your body language! That's how it is. You don't have to train a dog to wag its tail. If it's happy, it will wag its tail.

If you are happy, you don't have to pretend and smile, and put your hands in the right place, and stand in the right way.

FIND OUT

So how should you be? You should be *you*. And because you don't know, you sometimes wonder who you are.

Find out. The answers are in your heart. You are so fortunate that you have the temple of temples inside you. It is no ordinary temple. Here resides the *undebatable*, the formless, the genderless. The one who has never had a birthday or a funeral. You are the vessel that can make it possible. This is your time in which your cup can be filled.

Look for it. Fill your cup, however you can do it. That's the mission.

The human drama goes on. But amidst this human drama is a dance that is so exquisite. There is a lot of noise in the world, but there is also a song that is being sung. There are a lot of rhythms in the world that are out of sync. But there is one rhythm that is playing perfectly.

There is an exquisite rhythm of the breath coming in and out. And in this, you are blessed with the gift of life. Not tomorrow. Today! Who are you? And why do you need to know? Because this is the only way you will be able to tell the difference between the truth and the lies.

How do you know today was made for you? Because a day will come that will *not* be made for you. Would you like any other proof? If today came and you were here, it was made for you. And you always thought it was made for somebody else, right? You always thought, "Well, what can I do about it? It's here." No. It was made for you. Because one day will come which will not be made for you, and you will not be able to do anything about it. All your money, your intellect, your experience, will do nothing.

THE AWARD

We have a lot of pride. And we should have pride. But our pride should be in the fact that we are alive today. We have been blessed. We have been given a gift. We have been given an award. No award can be bigger than life.

This award, this gift of life, is yours. Yours. This day was made for you. And there will be another day coming that is made for you. And another day will come that is made for you. Get ready. Because when you start accepting those days that are made for you, then you're going to start living, thriving, being a human being. Not somebody going around saying, "I believe in that. I believe in this."

When you think you have broken a bone, you still want to believe it's not broken. But that doesn't help, does it? That's why you go to the doctor and say, "Take an x-ray." And the doctor looks at the x-ray and says, "No, it's not broken." Now you *know* it's not broken. And if it's broken, you know it's broken.

You need to know. You don't do well with believing. Look at the world. Very little knowing, a lot of believing, and it doesn't work.

Remember the people I mentioned who get used to the smell from the paper mill? When will you know a stench is a stench? When you smell the fresh air.

> How do you know today was made for you? Because a day will come that will not be made for you.

A wedding takes place
when a human being is born.
It's a very special wedding
of the infinite and the finite.

ATTEND YOUR OWN WEDDING

THERE IS SOMEONE YOU CAN LIVE WITH HAPPILY EVER AFTER. THAT ONE IS IN YOUR HEART.

We have become the society of what we don't have. People want to be millionaires, billionaires, even "trillionaires." What happened to cause the financial crisis? So much greed, so much anarchy. People blatantly telling lies and everybody believing. And not after having made one million, after billions!

We do not dream about what we have, we dream about what we *don't* have: "Oh, I wish I could have that." "I wish I could do this." Why? We have forgotten our own possibility.

RICH, SMART, STRONG

If you want to be rich, all you have to do is be generous. If you want to be smart, all you have to do is be simple. If you want to be strong, all you have to do is be kind.

Who does not have kindness in them? Everybody's born with kindness. It's free. And if you have that kindness, you can be strong.

Everybody wants to look smart. "Oh, yes, I know this and I know this and I know this." If you want to be smart, just be simple and you will be the smartest. Do you have simplicity in you, or do you have to go to a shop and say, "I will take ten dollars worth of simplicity"? No. You have it in you. But do you think simply? No.

Look at the condition of the world. It's not very pretty. Some people turn to God. What has happened in the world? Is it God's doing or our doing? We did it. But we are saying, "God, *you* fix it!" We are no longer living in the world of reality, we live in the world of beliefs.

So, in your life, what do you know? Do you know the simplicity that is inside you? Do you feel the peace that is inside you? Have you felt the riches that are inside you? Have you understood the wisdom that is inside you?

Do you know about your own rhythm? Do you know about your own life?

WHAT IS YOURS?
You may say, "Life is very complex." Is it complex, or have you *made* it complex? You say things like, "That's my uncle." "That's my house." "That's my wife." "That's my job." "That's my husband." "That's my car." These things are not yours.

Some people say, "This is my body." Is it? It'll be left behind. People might bury it, people might burn it. It'll go back into the soil. It'll be recycled.

If you want to be rich, be generous.

If you want to be smart, be simple.

If you want to be strong, be kind.

There's not that much new stuff that shows up on this earth. Everything that's here is basically recycled. So are you. You want to know what you were in your last lifetime? You could have been an eggplant. A tomato. Not very profound, huh? You would like it better if I said, "Oh, you were an emperor." Chances are, you were probably an eggplant, a cucumber. Maybe a pine tree. Who knows? And who cares?

I don't. Because I know I should be caring about now. Do we care about now? No. We care about yesterday: "He said that to me." "Oh my God! He did something very bad to me!" Yesterday, we care about. And do we care about tomorrow? Absolutely. We are all enamored by tomorrow: "What's going to happen?"

Here is a big statement, and it's very profound: "Whatever it is that you are looking for is inside you." Why is it profound? Well, how does the person who made this statement know what you are looking for? Isn't it a huge assumption that we are all looking for the same thing? But could it be that we are all looking for the same thing? We may call it different names. Some people call it "peace." Some people call it "God." Some people call it "joy."

There's only one well, and everybody comes to this well to fetch the water. Somebody brings a bucket, somebody brings a clay pot, somebody brings a metal pot, somebody brings a decorated pot. The pots may be different, but the water is exactly the same, because it comes from the same well.

THE WEDDING

We cannot thrive on our differences forever. Differences are good and differences should be appreciated, but they should not be the basis of our functioning in the world. You look a little different than me. Good. Nice. It is easy to recognize you and easy to recognize me. But don't forget that we all came from the same place and we landed on the same place: Port Earth. Could it be we all have the same mission? I think so. And the mission is to be fulfilled.

Whatever you are looking for is inside of you.

A wedding takes place when a human being is born. It's a very special wedding of the infinite and the finite. The finite stays finite, the infinite stays infinite. But for the period of this wedding, this dance, this show, this existence, the two are coming together. Do you understand what has happened? In this finite human, the infinite has come. Not for very long, mind you.

But here's the wedding. And what is the possibility? To feel joy. What is so big about joy? When you feel joy, you light up. You don't have to be reminded to smile. It comes automatically. You become content. You become you. You become rich. You become kind. You become conscious. You become real. You become a human being.

Is there any doubt when a grape is ripe? It is plump. It is ready to explode. It is at that point where the skin is so tight that the grape shines. And maybe it even develops a little crack with a little of its juice running out.

When you are in peace, when you understand, when you celebrate this wedding, then you, too, shine. You begin to bloom.

UNIQUE

Human beings are not horribly wicked. They have so much sweetness in them. But maybe the party never happened. And maybe it is time for that party to begin. Every human being has that kindness, has that possibility. But maybe you have never been invited to your own wedding. If you want, I can help you so you get to attend your own wedding. Because you should. It's the chance of a lifetime.

Will it happen again? Not this one. Do you realize how unique you are? I have heard people say, "Oh, I'm just an ordinary guy." No, you're not. Your DNA is incredibly unique. Do you know that? And in this human temple, the divine has come. Not "Is maybe coming." Has come! The divine has arrived.

Where does this human life come from? The saga begins with the first breath in. That's how we begin, all of us. Breath in. Not *out*. In! And it'll go on like that: in, out, in, out; till one day, it won't be in. It'll be out. You will take the last breath. And it'll go out, not in. And each breath that comes in and goes out forms a beautiful swing. Who is swinging this swing?

Do you know that the coming of this breath is your blessing? "No, no," you say. You want a car.

We dream about what we don't have, because we have forgotten our own possibility.

A man on his bicycle going to the office is slightly late and is praying, "Please, God, help me to get to the office at the right time." And the guy who has just opened up a little bicycle repair shop is also praying to God: "Please send me someone who's got a flat tire." And God must be turning his head left and right like the people watching the tennis match.

HAPPILY EVER AFTER

This is our shortsightedness, because we have been caught up in the Cinderella story. "And they lived happily ever after" is not a real story. "Happily ever after" between two people is impossible, unless one of them is dead.

The man falls in love. And of course, in the beginning, the girlfriend is very careful not to show him anything ugly. And the man is very careful to make sure she sees nothing unsightly. So every time: shave, use cologne, comb the hair. And "Here are the flowers."

Then comes "I do." And a week after that the man sees his wife and she looks like an alien. The curlers are like little antennas with hair

You want a cute girl. You want a nice man. This is what you pray for. On TV, I've seen the soldiers going to fight in Afghanistan. They all huddle together and say, "God, give us the strength to defeat our enemy." And then, a few kilometers away, there are all their enemies. They're also praying to God: "Give us the strength to beat those guys."

Have you seen a tennis match on TV? The ball goes back and forth. Have you looked at the audience? They are turning their heads left and right, left and right. God must be doing the same thing.

wrapped around them. She's walking around in an old bathrobe; no makeup. And she looks at her husband. He's got a straggly beard, a big zit on his face, hairs poking out where they shouldn't be, and the bald spot is obvious. And she thinks, "I married that?"

But reality is much more beautiful than a fantasy, much more beautiful than *any* fantasy. Because there is someone that you can live with happily ever after, and that is the one that is in your heart. No conflicts. No judgment. This is the true reality.

You are here, and you are the ocean of peace, of kindness, of understanding, of happiness. Look within, and you will see what I am talking about.

I am not telling you how you can eliminate problems in your life. But I can tell you about a way not to be affected by the problems. I am not telling you how to stop the rain. But I can tell you about an umbrella to use so you don't have to get wet every time it rains. That's what I do. And it is my honor and my privilege to tell you that you are missing nothing, that you have everything.

KNOW

The only problem is, you don't know you have everything. And you might live your whole life thinking, "Oh, poor me! What bad cards Fate dealt out to me!" But it's a full deck, not a half deck, not a quarter deck—a full deck. Let me show you a game you will win every time. It is the game of life, the game of understanding, the game of knowledge. Not a river of beliefs. There's nothing wrong with believing, but knowing is much better.

So know. Enjoy. Know you are blessed. You may be saying, "Give me proof." The proof is, you are alive.

You are missing nothing. You have everything. The only problem is, you don't know that.

BOMBARDMENT

BOMBARDMENT
BOMBARDMENT

TECHNOLOGY IS BOMBARDING US DAY AND NIGHT. WANT TO BE BOMBARDED BY SOMETHING ELSE?

There is a lot that is good in all our lives. But we have certain habits that are not so good. One of the bad habits is that we are attracted to distractions. As the word "distraction" implies, one would think that we wouldn't be attracted to it, but we are. Any little distraction somewhere, and that's where our attention goes.

That's a bad habit. It robs you of the essentials that you need to make your life a beautiful occasion. Because this is the possibility: You can make one lifetime—one lifetime—the most incredible time.

How? Time is time. You can't accelerate it, and you can't slow it down. You are in this world, you exist. One day you weren't; today you are; and one day you will die. I have said this many, many times, but very few people understand what it means, because of the distractions. When the time comes that you lose the capacity to be distracted—and such a time does come—then you begin to understand what life is about.

EXCITEMENT OR JOY?

Look at anyone's life. Some people think bungee jumping is exciting. To actually challenge death; climbing a vertical rock without any safety lines, just their fingertips and powder: "Take me on, Death!"

And the only reason Death *doesn't* take them on is because Death is laughing so hard. Bowled over. Tears running down the face. Almost to the point of hypoxia.

32

All that's standing between them and dying ends when Death sobers up. And when that happens, they're gone. They find themselves not close to nature, but *in* it. As manure. As their bodies rot and become dirt again.

So what is life about? Is it about excitement? Or is it about having a heart full of joy?

All the things that we think are important will one day turn around and become unimportant. I have been reading letters from people who are either at the front of the line or two or three people from the very front. We're all in that line. Everybody is headed that way. The law of existence states that you are here but for a limited time. And no one—no one—gets to break that law.

Some people say, "But there's cryogenics." Excuse me, Mr. Cryogenics. This universe is made out of dust. The earth is made out of dust. That metal cylinder that holds

the cryogenic agent and your head is made out of dust. Dust compressed, that's what it is. And the innate vulnerability of that compressed dust makes it highly probable that it will go back into the state of dust. Dust doesn't think. All it would take to end life on earth is that some dust from the universe heads this way, gets a little too close and is pulled toward the earth. And if that happened, it could obliterate this planet.

This planet that we live on is so fragile. In India, they put leaves of gold or silver over dishes of foods. These leaves are so delicate that if you breathe the wrong way they'll just go all over the place. This is how delicate our life is.

DUST TO DUST

From this dust many, many things have been created. Like the mountains. We refer to a mountain as something stable. This is the "snail/fly" scenario. Flies see at such a fast rate that when you try to kill them they see you coming in slow motion. A fly will sit there still cleaning its face, and to the fly, it's like, "What's the hurry? This slowpoke is going to take forever to get here. And in that time, I can have sex, lay eggs, all of that stuff." So when you are finally completely centered and ready to strike, for the fly, it's like, "Okay, time to take off." Nice, slow takeoff, and it's gone. And you say, "I missed it! I can't believe I missed it!" Of course you missed it!

Snails, on the other hand, see at such a slower rate that they don't even see you when you walk by. By the time the snail refreshes its field of vision, you're gone.

A long time ago when they first started taking pictures, the exposure times were too long to catch anything that was moving. The only things that could be captured on film were static things, like buildings. So they came to the conclusion that living things with souls could not be photographed. They were wrong, but it's the same thing for us. We see at a certain rate, and we don't see the mountain moving. Geologists, in their terms, "see" the mountains moving. If we had the frame rate to see it, we would be able to watch the Himalayas destroying themselves; because they are slowly eroding. That is the nature of dust.

Don't be caught up in frame rates. That is distorting your perception. A snail isn't slow, it is clipping along. Probably thinking it's moving so fast that it needs goggles. You can imagine one snail saying to the other one: "Man, slow down!" The flies? "Man, the world moves so slow!" This is the dilemma of frame rates. Don't be caught in frame rates. Your life perceived at a different rate goes by just like a snap of the fingers.

All the things that we think are important will one day turn around and become unimportant.

I am telling you something that I have been telling people all my life: Don't let another day go by without being touched by the magic inside you.

34

Don't let another day go by without feeling the fulfillment of the heart. Don't let another day go by that is filled with doubt, anger, and confusion. For someone who holds so much clarity within themselves, it is inexcusable to be in confusion even for one second.

THE JOURNEY AND THE OCEAN

The journey of life is like sailing across an ocean. Sometimes the waves get big. And what do you do when the problems become so insurmountable that you find you don't have all the strength you thought you had?

It's not a joy ride where you can just say, "Okay. That's enough. I'm going to pull over." No. If you go back, you've got to go through the same waves; if you go forward, you've got to go through the same waves.

In the grind of this ocean, the good and bad is like a wheel. It keeps going, keeps coming; keeps going, keeps coming. What precaution have you taken? That's the question.

The size of the wave is not under your control, but the precaution you can take is under your control. When you have found a way to be able to anchor yourself in the breath, then you have taken proper and correct precautions.

This is possible: You can find your home in the breath. Indeed, you can find your reality in the breath.

It's a matter of perception. It is through your perception that you see something that is fake as so real. The illusion—that is why it is an *illusion*—appears so real.

When everything goes bye-bye, you can't even get out of the chair, and the bathroom seems far away.

The nature of this world is to leave you with nothing. As you get older, everything starts going "Bye-bye. Bye-bye!" Do you know that? Eyesight? "Bye!" Teeth? "Bye!" Legs? "Bye!" Hearing? "Huh?" What do you become? You become like a baby. Sleep. Sleep. Sleep.

Beauty? "Bye!" Children? "Bye." And your friends? If they are your age, which is usually the case, well, they'd love to be with you if they could only get up from their chair. So friends? "Bye!" Prestige? What prestige? Wealth? "Bye!" No more job. Pension? Going mostly to the doctor.

At that point, when everything goes bye-bye, you can't even get out of the chair, and the bathroom seems far away.

I received a letter from a person who was at the very front of the line saying "I still have what you have shown me inside of me. And that's everything." This is the difference there can be in a person's life, and that's what you need to understand: you can be saved from the trauma of having nothing.

BOMBARDMENT

Do you realize how much we are being bombarded? Everybody's got their gadgets. Technology is bombarding us day and night. When was the last time you really had five minutes not being involved in thinking about something?

These gadgets have to-do lists. And all you do is think about the to-do list. "Have I put this in the to-do list? Have I put that in the to-do list?" You need a to-do list for the to-do list! Before, if you didn't want to open your mail, you didn't open your mail. Now you don't have a choice. It's there, wherever you go. People go for a walk, the "evening constitutional." And they're likely to get run over by a bus because they're too busy talking on their mobile phone, and so is the bus driver! And the joke would be if they were both cousins talking to each other. "Hang on a minute, I just got run over by a bus." "Hang on a minute, I just ran somebody over with my bus."

Bombardment, bombardment. And what does it bring you? Heartaches, confusion. Heartaches, confusion.

Want to be bombarded? Then be bombarded by clarity. Be bombarded by consciousness. Be bombarded by the feeling of being anchored in your breath. Focus on that. Nothing else should worry you because anything else that worries you will be a noose of death around your neck.

Don't let another day go by without being touched by the magic inside you.

ASKING THE RIGHT QUESTIONS

WHAT ARE THE QUESTIONS THAT WILL LEAD TO CLARITY ABOUT WHAT IT MEANS TO BE ALIVE?

The question "Why am I alive?" was first asked thousands of years ago. Millions of books have been written since that time. And nobody has come up with the answer. People are still asking the same question. In my opinion, there are only two kinds of people: those who have asked the question, and those who haven't asked it yet. Sooner or later, everybody will ask, "What am I doing here?"

Many people ask questions like "Where is God?" And there are a lot of answers. "Oh, he lives up there." "He lives in this place where there are clouds; where the gate is golden; where the temperature is perfect."

All these answers are based on speculation. But maybe if the right question was asked a real answer would come that is not a speculation, not a definition. And the right question to ask is not *where* God is, but "What is this existence?" If you could start looking into the answer for that, you would find that obviously God is not in some clouds, but God resides in your heart, within you.

KNOW-HOW

There are many traffic signs in a city: "Turn left," "Turn right," "Stop," "Go." And all the stop lights. Even electronic signs telling you the temperature. But you never see a sign that says, "The sun is shining." Why not? Because it's too obvious.

If you don't know how to fly an airplane and you're having a conversation with somebody who also doesn't know, you can have that conversation as long as you want. Because one person can say, "I think the airplane flies because it has a tail." And the other can say, "No, no, no. The most important part of the airplane is the wing. That's why there are two of them. In case one falls off, you still have another one. But an airplane only has one tail, so it can't be very important. If it falls off, nothing happens, right?"

What will help that conversation? There's only one thing that possibly can help: somebody who has the *know-how*. Because this conversation has no head, no tail, no ideas, no meaning, no beginning, and literally no end. It is as infinite as stupidity itself.

But know-how changes that in an instant. Somebody who knows can tell them, "Yes and no. An airplane only has one tail, but it is required, because it is what controls the direction and makes sure the airplane doesn't go into what they call 'flat spin'. And the airplane does not actually have two wings, left and right. It's just one wing sticking out of both sides of the fuselage. And the whole wing is necessary in order to fight gravity, because it creates lift." End of discussion.

We try to speculate about the very things whose inspiration comes from within us. We have defined what is good; we have defined what is bad. When things are going my way, that is good. When things are not going my way, that is bad.

KARMA

We have defined what it means to be happy and what it means to be unhappy. People say, "Happiness is when you have this and when you have that." And then when people get all those things and they're still not happy, they say, "What happened?"

Some people say, "It must be karma." Karma is a wonderful way to explain everything. You know why? Because it's a conversation between two people who have no idea what they're talking about. None!

Now how can I say this? You know where I was born? I was born in India. And everywhere I go in India, people expect me to support this idea of karma. And I don't! Because I have been told I was an emperor in my last lifetime. And it means nothing to me. I cannot go to the bank and say, "You know who I am? Give me all the money you have, and don't expect it back, because I'm the emperor."

I cannot go to Luxor in Egypt and say, "I used to be a pharaoh. All this is mine. Empty these palaces, I'm moving in." I cannot go to China and say, "I was the emperor. This is where I will stay now, in the emperor's palace." I would be thrown in jail so fast.

PRESENT!

I talk about the importance of breath. If you understand, you will benefit immensely. What is the importance of breath? Breath is the blessing that comes and allows the process of life to exist. What is life? Your presence on this beautiful earth. Your presence, that's what life is.

How can you be absent? If you don't understand this, that means you are absent! Did this life happen before? Does it matter? Seriously, does it matter? Will it happen again? Seriously, does it matter?

When you went to school, the teacher used to take attendance in the class by calling your name. And when you would hear your name, you would say, "Present!"

Did this life happen before?
Seriously, does it matter?

Will it happen again?
Seriously, does it matter?

I feel that every day I awaken there is a roll call. And in this roll call, I want to say, "Present!" Yes, I'm here today. I don't know how it happened, but I am here today. And it matters to me that I am here today. To me, it matters!

39

Every day there is a roll call. And I want to say, "Present!"

I don't know how it happened, but I am here today.

Because I also know that once upon a time, the answer to this question would have been "Absent." I wasn't here. And I also know that one day the answer to this question is going to be "Absent."

CONTENTMENT
What I have in my life that is truly mine is today. So you may say "But I can't do everything that I want today. What if I want to go to a beautiful place with a beautiful ocean and a beautiful

beach, and maybe I don't have the money? Maybe I don't have the time?"

Yes, maybe there are things that you cannot do today, or tomorrow, or ever. But there is one thing that you *can* do today, and tomorrow, and the day after that, and the day after that, and every day for the rest of your life, that neither the society, nor your friends, nor the people, governments, nor a lack of resources will ever stop you from achieving. You know what that is? It's being content.

You can be content today and nobody can take that away from you. All the people who feel victimized by the world should remember this. Nobody can steal your contentment away from you. You can abandon it yourself, but nobody else can take the happiness of the heart away from you. No one.

In America, there is a television show. I watched it once, and I thought it was incredibly intriguing. It's called—you know that big monster lizard, Godzilla? Well, this show is called *Bridezilla*. And it portrays these brides who are getting married, and they are the brides from hell. They're the most discontented people on earth— on their wedding day!

In the show, everything goes wrong. It's just a disaster. To them, the focus is not on getting married. The focus is the cake. The focus is the photographs. The focus is the music. And the poor husband is almost saying, "What am I doing?" You see—or hear—the hesitation when the time comes: "Do you take this . . ."

What I have in my life that is truly mine is today.

When everything else becomes the focus, rather than what the focus should be, it is the recipe for disaster. When you're driving on the road and you're focusing on the stereo system, or your cell phone, and you're not focusing on the road, on the traffic, on the obstacles, what's going to happen? A disaster.

Isn't that what happens in our life when we're not paying attention to what we're supposed to be paying attention to?

What are you supposed to be paying attention to? To the things that are important to *you*. And what are the things that are important to you? Now we come back to asking the right question. When you ask the right question, you will get the answer that will take away doubt; that will take away confusion and bring clarity. Ask the wrong question, and the answer you will get is not even worth hearing. And what will it do? It will increase your confusion. And you will have another question and another question and another question.

When a person dies, they put makeup on them to make them look good. In fact, they make them look really healthy. Red lips, a beautiful complexion, even a haircut if the person needed one. And they dress them up, sometimes in a tuxedo.

PEACE IS NOT A PAINTING

Now this person looks like the picture of living health. You think they're going to get up and start walking around? I mean, they look healthy. People even say, "He looks like he's sleeping. What could possibly be wrong with this person?"

There is one thing that is as wrong as it could possibly be: this person is dead! Painting him to make him look healthy will not bring him back to life. I wish that was a solution. We wouldn't need hospitals. You're sick? No problem. We will just paint you healthy.

But that's exactly what people do. All they do is basically paint their face. Put this on here, put that on there, have nice long hair, and smile. And you are a "man of peace"!

Some people say, "Stop all the wars and everything will be fine." That's like painting a dead person. There is something that caused the war. If that's not in peace, the war will come again and again, and again.

Some people think that peace means *quiet*. But imagine you are flying in an airplane and all of a sudden you crash in the middle of the Saharan desert. Everybody is dead, the plane is wrecked. You're the only person alive. And it's really quiet. Nobody to make noise. There isn't even a camel for hundreds of miles around you.

Would you really say, "Wow, it's so peaceful"? No. You will be wondering how you are going to survive for the next five minutes. "Everybody's dead! Oh, my God, the heat! Where is the water?" It's quiet.

Isn't it peaceful? No. Peace is much more than quiet. Much, much more.

People go to see a sunset. "Oh, this is so peaceful." I hear people say that all the time. And I don't have to say, "But it's not. It's not." They obviously like it. Fine. Let them enjoy it.

But peace is a state in which you are in equilibrium. Not upset, but in equilibrium. Where there is clarity, not confusion. Where there is an understanding, not doubt. Where you understand without questions, because you have felt. That's the only time you can say, "Yes, I have peace!" Because you have felt it.

Peace is a state in which you understand without questions.

And peace is not something you feel once in your life and say, "That's enough." Can you imagine if that was the rule? You have your pasta once in your life, that's it! You don't have to eat again? No. Not only do we eat every day, we make it tasty every day, so we can enjoy it.

THE PROCESS OF KNOWING

I have seen the best of cooks. They're cooking, cooking, cooking, and then they taste. I don't think it's a very sanitary habit, but sometimes they'll take their finger and dip it, and then put the finger in the mouth.

That one taste verifies all actions that the chef did. No questions need to be asked. No debate needs to be had. No ruling has to take place. No looking in a reference book is needed. None of that. Taste, and it's done.

This process is called *knowing*. You have seen people preparing to climb a ladder. They grab it, shake it, make sure it is sturdy. Can't they see it's sturdy? No. They can see it's there. But whether it is sturdy or not comes from feeling it.

Why are you alive? You'll never know the answer in words, but you can feel it.

THE HUMAN CONDITION

The human condition is, one day you are sitting in your living room and a thought comes to you. "I don't think this is my house." So you get up and leave the house in search of your house.

You look and you look and you look. And there are people who are going to say, "What does your house look like?" And you say, "It has a roof, it has windows, it has a door." Oh yes, but so do all the other houses.

There are only very few who are going to say, "You were in your house. Go back to where you were!" That takes knowing; that takes clarity. And not everybody has that clarity.

Those who search need to understand one thing: the desire for peace comes from within, and the fulfillment of this desire also lies within. The desire to be happy comes from within, and happiness also lies inside, not outside.

If you look to the outside for everything, including your peace and your happiness, you will be disappointed. Because it cannot come from outside. So the question is, are you willing to turn within?

When you do, you'll find the answer, and the answer will come in a feeling. You'll feel what you're doing here. Once you experience the joy, it will become clear to you why you are here. Once you experience the peace, it will become abundantly clear to you why you are alive.

Ask the right question. Get the right answer.

When you turn within, you'll find the answer, and the answer will not come in words. You'll feel what you're doing here.

43

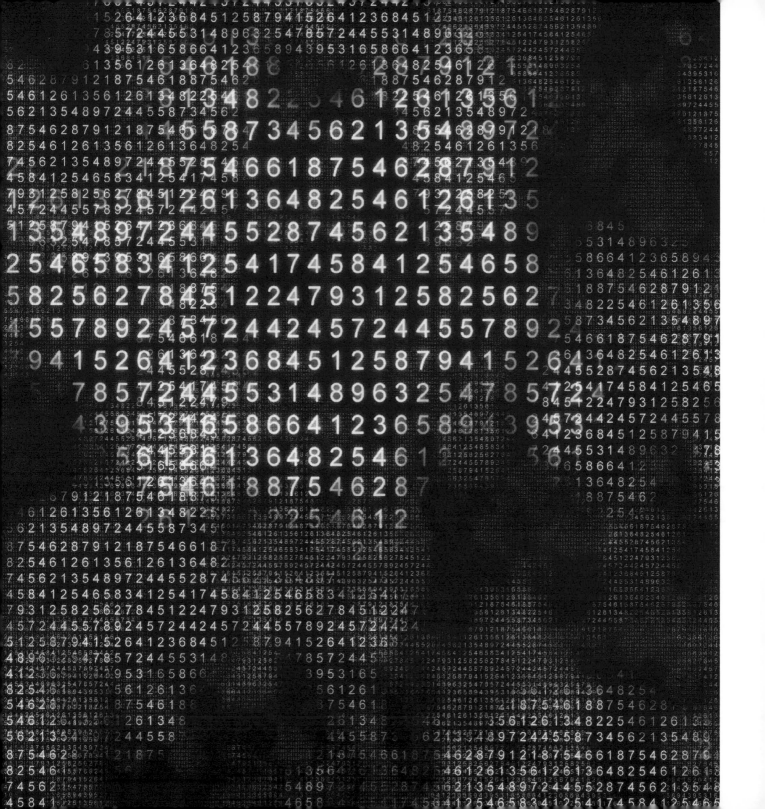

PART TWO

THE RICHNESS

Peace for just one day
is not richness.

But peace in abundance,
every single day,
every moment:
that is being rich.

THE DANCE OF THE DROP

SEE YOUR LIFE THROUGH THE EYES OF THAT WHICH GAVE IT TO YOU.

One day I decided to photograph drops of water, captured just as they were falling. I got a tray, I got some water and set up a system so that the water would fall, creating drops. I set up my camera and set up my flashes. It took almost all day to tweak it and set it up perfectly. And then I began to take pictures.

I had to wait and wait, watching the drop building up. And then it would begin to fall. And you want to capture it at its most glorious moment, which you have to do manually. And one after another after another, I would shoot and shoot.

Why am I telling you this? Because you, too, are a drop. Each human being on the face of this earth is a drop. And like any other drop, you will drop.

So what is this all about?

This is what it's all about: The drop is going to drop. We can't change that. We're not going to make it drop faster and we're not going to make it drop slower. But while this drop exists, there is a magnificence. And we can capture the magnificence of this drop. And then there will be an admiration that you could have *never* imagined, because it is so beautiful.

IMAGINARY WORLD

You lose yourself every day in an imaginary world. Have you ever heard this statement: "You are so beautiful that I have no words to describe your beauty"? I'm sure you've tried it on a few girlfriends or boyfriends.

Excuse me. You don't have words to describe this person's beauty, and you call that real? Two people walk up the aisle, and they are going to pledge themselves to each other for the rest of their lives. And there is a third person standing there who is telling them what to say: "I take so-and-so to be my lawfully wedded wife, to love and to hold and to cherish till I die."

You cannot even say to the person you're going to spend the rest of your life with what you want to say? You have to have a third person say it! And that's not an imaginary world? Believe me, there have been a lot of marriages and a lot of divorces. And divorce doesn't have to be on paper. The heart is the only place a divorce needs to take place.

"I will love you for the rest of my life." Two days later, "Get out of my house." "Get out of my life!" "You've ruined my life!" Is that a real world?

Even in the pathetic fairy princess stories, it's supposed to be happily ever after. In *your* princely story, there is no happily ever after. But you say, "This world is so good to me; it's real." It's not.

WHOSE TIME?

Your reality is that you are a drop. And you might think that's so ordinary. "A drop? That's all I am? How could you define me as a drop?" But if you truly comprehend the magnificence of the drop, you would scream with joy, "I am a drop, I am a drop!" because you would understand.

Unfortunately, you count your life the wrong way—basically because you are a slave of the system. The system says, "This is how it is. There are 24 hours in a day." Have you ever questioned that? No. "A week is seven days." Have you ever questioned that? No. "A year is 365 days." Have you ever questioned a year? Never.

You were so excited when you got your first watch that you forgot to ask the most important question: "What is it going to tell me?" Is it really going to tell you about your existence? No. It is going to tell you time. What time? Whose time? When you look at your watch, what do you look at? "It's time to go to sleep." "It's time to wake up." "It's too early." "It's too late." Too early for what? Too late for what?

The drop got hold of a watch. And it was so caught up in trying to tell time, that it forgot all about its existence, its reality. Reality is a big word. Existence is even bigger. Truth—too big. But beauty, you can relate to. So let me put it this way: have you forgotten your own beauty, have you forgotten your own love, have you forgotten

47

**Have you forgotten
your own beauty,
your own love,
your own passion?**

your own passion, have you forgotten your own feeling of being this drop?

ONE LITTLE DROP

When this drop drops, incredible magic occurs. For a moment, the drop comes up again. No jet engines, no fuel, no wings. Just gravity and mass, and here it comes, and it hits the water and it splashes. It dances like a ballerina wanting the truest expression of oneness. For that one moment, it is all by itself. And then, before you can blink an eye, without a trace, it disappears. It becomes one with what it sprang from. That's it. Done. The show of one little drop of water is finished.

You, too, are a drop. One little drop of kindness. One tiny little drop of the ultimate blessing. You have forgotten how blessed you are. You look at other people and, if somebody has won the lottery, you say, "Oh, he's so lucky!" And then you say, "What about me, God?" You see somebody rich: "How come I don't have that?"

In God's eyes, that's not a gift. In God's eyes, letting you be a drop is the ultimate gift. When you look at a painting, you say things like, "Ah, I don't like it." "I like it." "I don't like this." "I like that." Next time you look at a painting, try to look at it from the painter's perspective. See that painting through the eyes of the person who painted it. See this life through the eyes of that which gave it to you, and you will see that it is the most amazing blessing that can ever be.

Some time ago, at an event, I said, "I'm talking about everyone's God." And I thought about it later. "Have I invented another one?" No. God doesn't need to be re-invented but to be *de-invented*. There are already too many inventions. We need to come back to the God of everyone, the one who everyone can pray to. Who everyone can like. Who judges no one. Who does not hold itself apart from the heart of any human being. Glad to dwell in you—with you—for the duration of this drop.

THE PHOTOGRAPHER

Do you know the rules of light? A thousand unlit candles cannot light even one candle, while one lit candle can light a thousand candles. It is not the size of the lamp that will remove the darkness. Even the smallest lamp can remove the darkness around it. So much of this universe is filled with darkness. Anywhere there is lack of light, it's dark, dark, dark, dark. And then one little lamp is lit. And it holds the darkness of the universe at bay. For *you*.

That is strength. That is power. All you need in your life is a light. The real light.

You go to a fair with your family to have a good time. And a photographer comes and says, "Do you want to have your photo taken?" So you can remember going there.

In the fair of life, you are very busy. You have this to take care of, you have that to take care of, you've got to do this, you've got to do that. And here comes the photographer. And some people don't know what to say to him. Some people say, "Okay." So he says, "Smile." And some people say, "No. I have nothing to smile about, just take the picture." Some people say, "No. Not today." But the photographer in the fair of life knows

49

you're a drop. You're not coming again and again. Because it is only in your make believe world that you get to come again.

GHOSTS AND ALIENS

People say, "Oh, well, in my last lifetime…" In America, they have TV shows about ghosts. And they have special cameras to capture the ghosts.

So one day I decided, "Okay. I'll watch the show. I'd like to see a ghost." I'm watching, I'm watching, I'm watching, and they're all like, "Oh, my God. Did you feel that?" And, "Did you see that?! Oh, my God! That moved!" After the whole thing was over, I said to myself, "*I* didn't see a ghost." What is this about? A world of make believe.

Snow White is lying in the coffin. She's been lying there for a long time. She wouldn't have brushed her teeth for a month. Morning breath is bad enough, so even if the prince was really attracted to her, as soon as he opened the lid of the coffin—imagine the smell of her breath after a month of no tooth brushing! But that's not what you imagine. You imagine the romance in the world of make believe.

Now what do some other people believe? "Oh, there must be somebody out there." I have had this conversation with people. It's hard to discuss. The universe is so big. But there are scientists who thought exactly that. And they still do. And so they set up a huge facility, scanning the universe for signals.

Now this is what's interesting. They haven't scanned everything—and I'm not saying there's nobody out there. Maybe there is. It's entirely possible. But they're still scanning, and by now they have scanned a fairly good chunk around the earth, actually a few light years. A light year is huge—*really* big. And they've scanned all that, and they found nobody. They've sent a probe out with pictures, sayings in different languages, and music. No answer. Nobody sent a message back saying, "Man, that music is cool! Can I download some more?" Nothing. Not even, "What was that all about? What did you say?" Nothing. So we're talking about light years and light years and light years, and there's nobody around but us. Just us. And that's official.

GREED

There is an incredible message in that: learn to get along with each other. There is no one else. No point in fighting. You are not impressing anyone.

Some people blame drought. No drought has killed as many people as people have. Other people blame plagues. No disease has killed as many people as people have. If there is a drought, it is the drought of compassion. If there is a disease, it is the arrogance of one person toward the other. And it still continues to play out. There are more educated people than there ever were, and people are still blaming God and their karma.

You, too, are a drop. One little drop of kindness.

The first economic downturn, whenever it happened, happened because of greed. The second one, greed. The third one, greed. The fourth one, greed. And the last one? Greed. And will there be more? Wish we could bet on it, because we would become very rich. Of course there will be more, and it's going to be because of greed. There's no shortage of greed in this world.

From Hieronymus Bosch's painting "The Seven Deadly Sins and the Four Last Things," circa 1500.

What people need
is a light in their life.
Without that lamp, all there is is
darkness. That's the other rule of light: without light, guaranteed darkness.

When you are in darkness, here comes greed: you're game. Here comes anger: you're game. Here comes fear: you're game. That's why I say, "Light the lamp."

Don't be a victim. You are but a drop, and you are magnificent. Do you want a picture? Then look your best and smile. Let the photographer take a picture you will remember for the rest of your life. Because that is how satisfaction is. That is how peace is. Peace does not need to be measured. "How long have I had peace? Five minutes? Six minutes?" No. Time doesn't matter when you are in peace. When you understand, it isn't *how much* you understand, but that you understand.

The first economic downturn happened because of greed. The second one, greed. The third one, greed.

Will there be more? Of course there will. There's no shortage of greed in this world.

The world gives you a compliment: "Oh, you look so beautiful today." And people say, "Oh, thank you!" Don't be mesmerized by this comment, because it is the same mouth that one day will make another comment: "You look old. What happened to you?" That's the nature of it.

A true compliment would be, "Recognize your inner beauty." That's a compliment. Inner beauty never gets old. It always looks beautiful.

THE DOORS OF THE HEART

Open the doors of the heart and feel what it feels like to be in this world with a heart full of gratitude. With light around you, not with confusion and doubts, but with clarity. Not with bewilderment, but in wonder.

When you look with the eyes of the heart—not with judgment, but with the eyes of the heart, you see the magnificence. We are too much into "I look fat," "I look skinny," "I look old," "I look young." What do you really look like? Look inside you and see the magnificence. It's so beautiful. So incomparable. So unbelievable.

How spectacular is this drop? It drops; it dances. And when it dances, you can't even say for how long—but it is magnificent.

Look inside you and see the magnificence. It's beautiful. Incomparable. Unbelievable.

ARE YOU IGNORING THE OBVIOUS?

IGNORING IGNORING

WHAT IS THE OBVIOUS? THAT YOU ARE ALIVE. THAT YOU ARE UNIQUE. THAT WHAT YOU'RE LOOKING FOR IS INSIDE YOU.

There was a doctor. He knew that when Death came, Death was only allowed to take one person. That was the rule. So he worked very hard to make an identical duplicate of himself. When the time came, he lay down and he put the duplicate right next to him. Death came. "What's this?" Death knew he could only take one. But there were two of them. So the doctor was lying there as still as he could. And Death was in a quandary. "My goodness. Who do I take? I can't make a mistake."

So Death thought and thought and then said, "Doc, I've got to hand it to you. You're the best. You even fooled me. My hats off to you. But you made a mistake."

The doctor's lying there thinking, "What mistake could I possibly make? I'm the best!" And as much as he tried to resist, he said, "What mistake?" And Death said, *"That!"*

The doctor took everything into account: The look, the skin, the feel. Had he been humble and kept his mouth shut, Death would have left empty-handed. But he had no humility.

How much humility do we need? Just enough to get along with ourselves. That's all. Because if you can get along with yourself, you can get

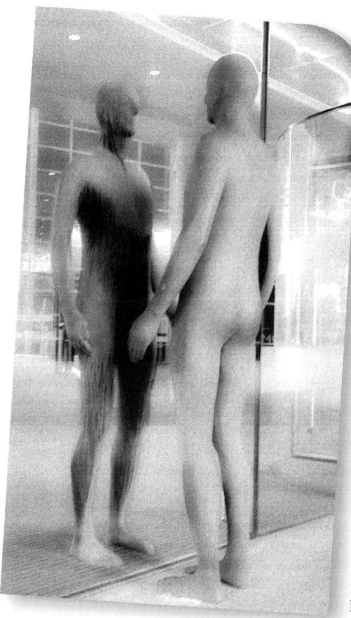

How much humility do we need? Just enough to get along with ourselves.

FLOWERS

Peace brings a lot of joy. It's beautiful, it is something we need. It's not an idea, it's not a luxury—it's a necessity. And the desire for peace comes from within every single human being.

It's like a garden. What makes a garden? The flowers. What is a flower? It is at once so delicate and so beautiful in its delicateness, you would think: What could it do, what could it accomplish? Amazingly enough, some of the flowers feed many. This little thing that only blooms for a short time has worked it all out—including its relationship with the sun that could destroy it. It feeds many, it attracts, it smells wonderful. Even its colors are particular for the insects that it wants to invite.

A seed is sown. It sprouts. It becomes a flower. And in this bloom it comes to its full potential, its full beauty. And that's what the flower is about. It's not about the sprouting and it's not about the wilting. It's about that bloom that is so attractive.

along with your neighbor. If you can get along with yourself, you can get along with another person. But if you can't get along with yourself, you can't get along with anybody.

In my opinion, we too are flowers. We too need to bloom. But in the garden where we exist, the flowers have come up with excuses for why they shouldn't bloom. "Ah, what's the point? We're all going to die one day. Just stay intact, forget about the blooming, forget about feeding anybody. Just bide your time and survive."

When I go around the world and talk about peace, it's like a gardener saying to the flowers, "Forget your excuses. Will you please bloom? Because that's when you are the most beautiful. That's why you are here: to bloom."

You can go to the moon, that's fine. If you go to Mars, that's fine, too. But you, as a flower, cannot forget to bloom. Because if you do, that is the greatest tragedy.

The gardener says to the flowers, "Will you please bloom?"

I tell you about yourself. I don't know your name, I don't know your occupation, I don't know where you live. I don't know when you were born. So am I qualified to tell you about yourself? I'll try, because I am no different than you, and perhaps you have the same aspiration that I do: to be fulfilled; to be in peace; to experience the ultimate expression of life, called joy.

TRUE SUCCESS

You know sadness. And you hate it so much you will do anything possible to avoid it. In fact, I think your definition of success really means successfully avoiding sadness. The whole insurance industry is based on that. You watch these commercials: "You know why I'm smiling? I lost my job." You're looking at the TV thinking, "You lost your job and you're smiling?" And then the commercial continues, "But I have insurance and it's paying for it."

Success for us becomes to avoid trouble and pain. Because nothing makes us more miserable than pain. But here is the twist: even if you successfully avoid pain, that doesn't necessarily mean you will have joy.

In a dark room, you cannot take a bucket and say, "I know how to get light in here. All I'll do is fill this bucket with darkness and throw it out the window and I'll keep doing that until there is light." That doesn't work. Light is a presence. Darkness is an absence. If you have secured a place in this world where you will not be bothered by problems, that doesn't mean joy will automatically say, "Here is a trouble-free zone. I'll go there." No. It won't.

The world gives this formula: build your life to ensure there will be no problems. But then there have been those others who have said: "Ensure there is *joy* in your life."

What does that mean? Smiling every minute? Is that what joy is? A lot of people look at these people who are "enlightened." They might wear saffron or white robes; they've got nice gray hair and maybe a colored mark on their forehead. When I see those "enlightened" people, I want to tell them a joke to lighten them up!

Do you know what "lighten up" means? It means "Don't be so heavy." But it could also mean light—as in "Lighten up!" Because inside of you are questions. But inside of you are answers,

too. Inside you is the possibility of feeling pain. But inside you is also the possibility of limitless joy. Do you know that you have no limit for joy? Your tolerance for pain is very small but your tolerance for joy is off the scale.

When you're having a good time, you don't say, "Stop this!" But when you are in pain, you say, "God, help me out!" This is who we are. Good and bad, right and wrong is not the issue.

What I'm saying does not affect your family, your business, your this, your that. You know you can be successful in your business and not be successful in your life. What I am saying is that if you truly want the ultimate success, you have to include both.

Do you not have the thirst to be fulfilled? Has nothing inside you ever stirred and said, "I want to be fulfilled too"?

If you can't get along with yourself, you can't get along with anybody.

LISTENING

I cannot tell you in one statement, "The purpose of your life is to be happy, to be in peace." That would be stupid, because it would be coming from me. It has to come from you.

We know how to hear. But we don't know how to listen. Listening is an art. If the politicians listened to people, this world would be different. If husbands listened to their wives, this world would be different. And, dare I say, if wives listened to their husbands, this world would be different. If parents listened to their children, this world would be different. And if children

57

could listen to their parents, this world would be different. But we don't listen.

When the call of the heart comes and says, "Be fulfilled!" we don't listen. We say, "Ah, I don't have time for this stuff. I'll try to make time…" This is the biggest misunderstanding there is. You have no control over time; time has control over you. You don't have time's number; time has got your number.

Look at the world. We've been placed on the most magnificent planet you can imagine. There isn't another one like this around for light years upon light years. And what are we doing? We are busy destroying it. Why? Because heaven isn't here, is it? We have to die to go to heaven. And that's the biggest drawback of heaven—that you have to die.

In this idea of heaven you will be judged to see whether you can go there or not. And this is how we look at God. God sits there saying, "Make a mistake. I am watching you everywhere 24/7. I am watching you 365—even in your dreams. You think about the wrong thing and you're going to have to answer to me."

YOU ARE THE ANGEL

But have you looked around? You *are* in heaven. A heaven that is more magnificent than any heaven that could be described. Every single day is different. Every cloud has a different shape. Every snowflake that falls is unique. And, yes, there are angels here on earth. Lots of angels. Seven billion of them. They just don't know it.

You are the angel that can set yourself free; to fly, to be, to exist. You are the one. You're waiting for one to come from the sky but it was pretty miraculous how you came. From nothing, all of a sudden, there you were. And your whole world started to change. You came out, you were blue. You took that first breath and the chemical signals were sent to your mother through the placenta saying, "No more blood; I am on my own. I'm here." The grand entrance.

Then all your life, this beautiful rhythm of the breath coming in and out. In, out, in, out. And you know how it ends? The symphony ends with your last breath out. Not in. Out.

And in this period from that first breath in to the last breath out, what is it all about? It is about the possibility of being content, the possibility of being fulfilled. It is about existing in heaven—here on earth.

"On earth!" People have given up on that part. "Oh, it's not possible. We're too greedy." You've got your eyes closed and you're saying, "What colors are you talking about?" Well, open your eyes. "What light are you talking about?" Open your eyes. "What possibility are you talking about?" Open your eyes. Give your heart a chance. Give yourself a chance. See. Listen to that rhythm inside of you.

> **You are the angel that can set yourself free; to fly, to be, to exist.**

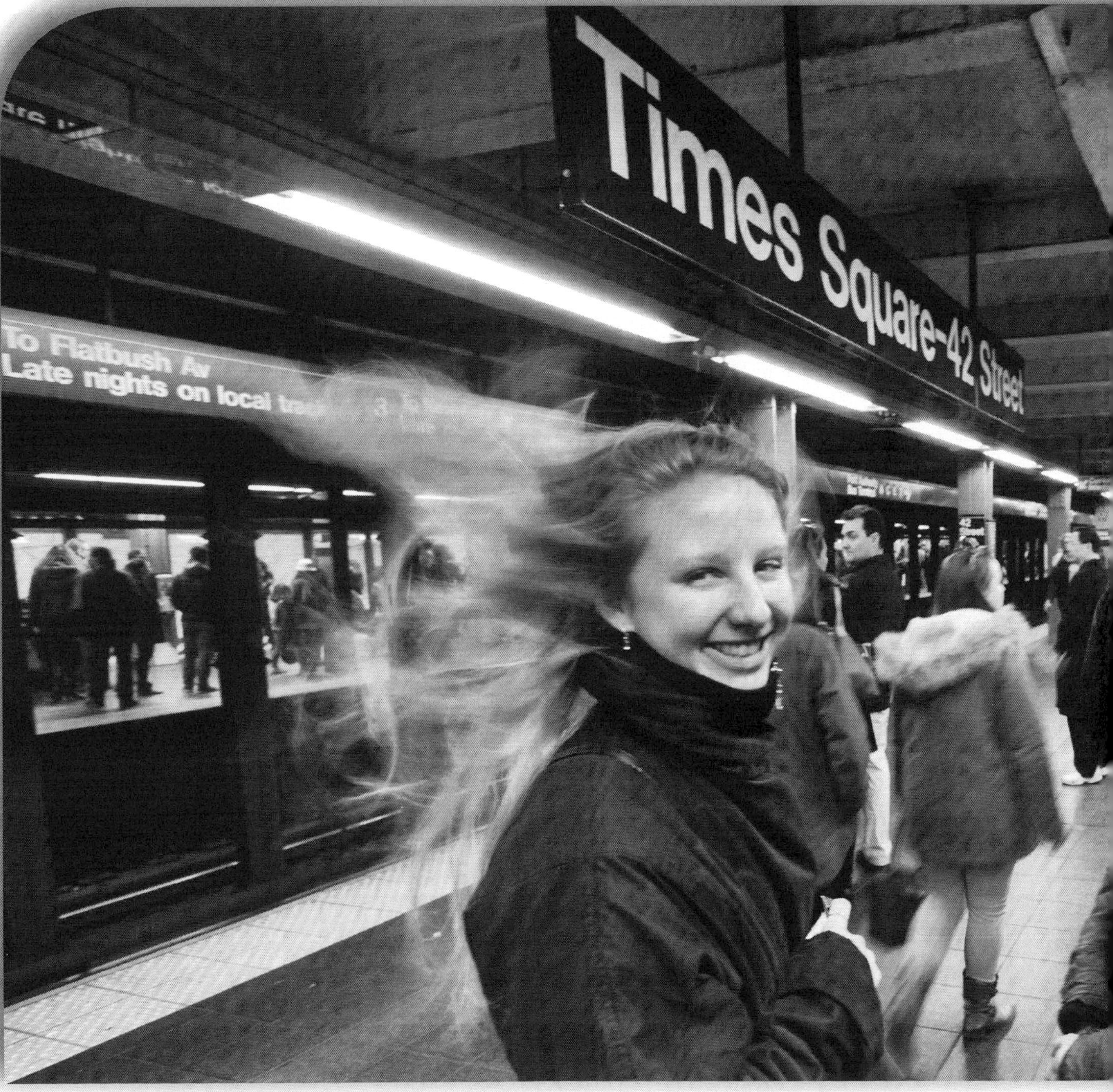
Times Square-42 Street
To Flatbush Av
Late nights on local

Something pushes you every day to be better and better. To be lighter and lighter. To be clearer and clearer. That something pushes you every day to be in that heaven, and has been doing so since you were a little child.

How could we ignore a voice that is so strong inside every human being, calling us to be fulfilled? How can you ignore it? What do you practice every day? Whatever you practice, you will get good at.

How could we ignore a voice that is so strong inside every human being, calling us to be fulfilled?

EXPECTATIONS

Do you practice frustration? If you do, you will get frustrated very quickly. All it takes is a horn honking. "Who honked at me?" You call your child, and the child doesn't come. "I said come here *right now!*" People walk into a restaurant, they sit down, and the waiter doesn't come. "What kind of restaurant is this?" Well, you're the one who walked in. We have our expectations, do we not? People come to me and they expect something from me, too.

They say, "Give me peace," and I say, "Sorry, it's already inside you." People say they're looking for peace. I say, "Why? You already have it."

People ask, "Where should I search?" Here's a clue: in you is the only place you have never looked. Because it is easier to believe that the answer will come from here, from there, from a book, from a session, from a course, from a school, from this, from that. But maybe nobody ever said to you, "What you are looking for is already inside you!" until you come across me, and I say, "Did you try that?"

So many people are afraid of knowing who they are. They say, "If I get to know myself, what if I find something terrible?" You have more reason to be scared of opening your drawer at home—there could be a snake in there—than looking within you. People really think darkness is an entity. They have been led to believe there is this thing called the devil. He's got a pitchfork, he wants you, and if you are a dropout he gets to have you.

Why? Some poet, a long time ago, was really ticked off at the pope of the time, so he wrote a drama about what would happen to that pope after he died: he would be boiled in oil. Since then, we have taken it upon ourselves to think, "I don't want to be boiled in oil."

Do you know that the sadness of this world and the pain some people suffer is a lot graver than being boiled in oil? When somebody jumps out of a window, can you imagine their state of mind, how much pain they must be in? If you offered them a choice of being boiled in oil, they'd say, "Thanks! When do we start?"

The reality is actually very simple. Next time you have any doubts that you are super blessed, take a breath. Because the breath that comes in and out of you is nothing short of the most incredible blessing. You are made out of different minerals and water and other elements. Do you know how much of that stuff is available on this earth? Lots. But of all that potential, you exist. Do you know you are unique? As unique as the snowflake. As unique as the flower. There's no one like you. And there will never, ever again be anyone like you.

The way you smile, the way you think, the way you laugh, the way you cry. The way you sleep, the way you're awake, the way you are when you are generous, the way you are when you're kind. The way you love, the way you receive, the way you understand. There will never, ever be another one like you on the face of this earth. Never. What does that mean to you?

IGNORANCE
You need to understand your preciousness. That's when you begin to know who you are. If somebody handed you a coin and said, "There is only one of these in the whole world," you would say, "Oh, my God! I'm so lucky to have this coin. Nobody else has one."

You yourself are unique and you are caught up with a coin! This is where awakening comes in, because we are sleeping a slumber of ignorance. We usually associate the word ignorance with being dumb, stupid. But the root of the word isn't something that means "stupid", it is to *ignore*. To ignore the obvious is the biggest kind of ignorance.

What is the obvious? That you are alive. That you are unique. That is obvious. That heaven is within you is obvious. That what you're looking for is inside you is obvious. That to remove the darkness you need to bring in the light is obvious. That peace is inside you is obvious. And that you are blessed beyond belief is obvious.

You are a flower. Please, bloom.

People ask, "Where should I search?" Here's a clue: in you is the only place you have never looked.

61

ARE YOU RICH?

WHAT DO YOU HAVE THAT IS PRECIOUS, AND IN ABUNDANCE? IT'S NOT MONEY, AND IT'S NOT DIAMONDS.

You can be rich in many things, not just in money. So what is the definition of being rich? Two elements are involved. One, you have to have something precious. What does precious mean? Something that is not ordinary.

And secondly, you have to have an abundance of it. Gold is precious, but having some gold the size of a hairpin isn't going to make you rich. You have to have lots of it. And the more you have, the richer you are. Both elements, the preciousness and the abundance, play off each other to make you rich.

So now the question becomes, are you rich?

LAYERS

What do you have that is precious, and that you have an abundance of? There is something—and it's not money, and it's not diamonds. It is another kind of wealth. The breath that comes in and out of you is incredibly precious. And not only is it precious—here's the beauty—it comes in abundance.

Its presence qualifies every human being in the world to be rich. And it is the most beautiful gift. Life is the most beautiful gift that we have been given.

What is life? There are many, many definitions. But look at it this way: it's a bunch of layered sheets. Only one sheet is real. The rest are translucent overlays on top of the one real sheet. And sometimes there are so many overlays that you lose sight of the real sheet.

So this is what I am talking about: you can lift those layers, one by one, and see that they're only the layers. Every layer is changeable; and every layer represents a change. The only thing that doesn't change is the basic layer.

We have our relationships, and our friends, and we have our ideas, and our jobs, and this happening, and that happening. And pretty soon, getting caught in all those layers, we forget what the basic layer is, what life is all about.

THE PIANO OF LIFE

Some pianos come with 88 keys—from the lowest to the highest note. All songs played on that piano will be contained within those notes. So somebody could tell you, "Mash all the keys at the same time and you will play every single song there is." Technically it's true—but it isn't. Why? Because it will not sound beautiful. It will have no emotion. A song is not just about playing the key, but also about the silence in between the notes. The silence is just as important as the notes. If you just kept playing *"ding-ding-ding-ding,"* you've got a fire bell, not a song.

If in your life you take all the notes and mash them together and say, "Yeah, everything is fine. I'm playing a song," you are sadly mistaken. It is no song. It's just a big *"clunk, clunk, clunk"* sound. So if your life doesn't seem quite right, you are not mistaken. It's not being played right. The song of life is about the sequence. It is about the silence. It is about the harmony. It is about the emotion.

A lot of people say, "I have to do this, I have to do that, I have to do this, I have to do that." I say, "No!" But I'm not telling you what you should do and shouldn't do. I'm only telling you that there is something that is already happening. The big *do* is already *doing!* And it is the source of immense joy when you have found not only the abundance, but also the preciousness of existence, of breath, of the gift that is coming in and out of you.

I'm sure some people are thinking, "But that's too simple." No, it's not. It is at once the simplest thing, and at the same time it is the most complicated. Because we human beings are not good at undoing.

They say if you are a man, you don't ask directions. It's below your dignity. You just keep getting lost. "It's okay, it's okay. We'll find it. Now I know where I am!" Getting lost is our expertise. And getting found? No. Egos come into play. Pride comes into play. "Me being lost? *Me!* Never!" Getting lost is easy. Getting found is undoing all the things you did that got you lost. Undoing them, you will find where you need to go.

FINDING THE RIGHT PERSON

Being confused is easy. All you have to do is listen to everyone. But finding the right person to talk to is very complicated. Once you find the right person, it will be easy—incredibly easy. But finding the person is difficult, because everybody has already told you how that right person should be.

They should be five feet high, six feet high, seven feet high. They should be Indian; they should be from Israel; they should be from China; they should be from Himalayas. They should not be wearing clothes; they *should* be wearing clothes. Should have long hair, should have short hair, white robes, off-white robes, slightly off-white robes; short-sleeve robes, long-sleeve robes, long this way, not just that way. Wool; no leather. Leather, but handmade, personally made; not from your average shoe store.

And obviously, if the person wears a watch they can't be the one. They should just *know* the time! And the wisdom of the person is not judged by what they say, but by how many times they close their eyes. See how confusing all this is?

Everything I have said is what people do. They say, "These are the characteristics of the person who is the true guide." And I say that the characteristic of the person who is a true guide is to show you the way. Isn't that what a guide is about?

Somebody to point out the obvious: that you are alive. Not what you can do, but the fact that you are alive, that therein lies the foundation of peace for you. Therein lies your treasure. Therein lies your clarity. Therein lies your understanding. Therein lies your peace.

Being confused is easy. All you have to do is listen to everyone.

Not in the complicated. Not in the duties. But in the richness, the abundance, the preciousness of what has been given to you. You have already been blessed with it. It is not that you lack anything. You never have lacked anything from the time that you came on the face of this earth into this journey of life. What do you think life is about? Coping with problems?

I don't pretend I have command of all the writings, all the spirituality. I don't. All I know, and all I say, is that knowledge of the self is more important than all the knowledge of the world.

ONE AND ZERO

I will put that in context. It's no different than the relationship of one and zero. If zero comes first, and then one, one stays one, zero stays zero. Add another zero? No change. Add another zero? No change. Add another zero? No change. You can add eight thousand zeros in front of the one. No change. One will stay one, zero stays zero.

And if you put one first? Then every zero takes on a meaning. Now one doesn't stay one. It becomes ten. Add another zero, and it becomes a hundred. Add another zero, and it becomes thousand. And so on, and so on, and so on. Knowledge of the self, first. And then, everything else.

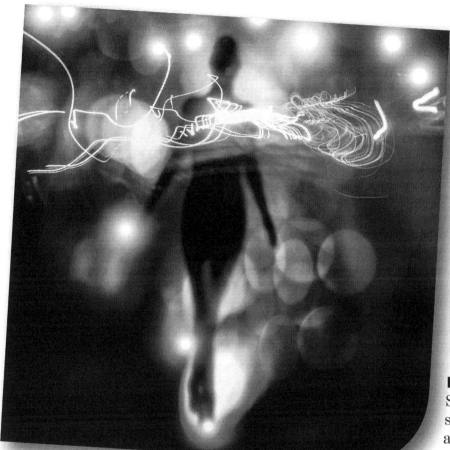

why there are so many zeros, and what they do—because all the zeros in the front don't mean anything.

You have to come first. It begins with you, your understanding, your life, your existence, your clarity, your song, your fingers on those keys that have been given to you—you playing a song. Not a hired artist. No, no, no. You playing the song. That's what it is about. It is your emotion that has to come out. It is your song. And it is your enjoyment of that song that means everything.

HEAVEN AND HELL

Some people might find this strange. "Why are you talking about *me*? Talk about other things. Talk about how we can all end up in heaven." There are a lot of good people who try to figure this out every day: "How are we going to end up in heaven?" They want reservations. They want confirmed reservations. They want to confirm their confirmed reservations.

There is a doubt, and it needs to be confirmed. There is no end to the confirmation process that is required, that after you die you'll really go to heaven. Now I'm telling you, "Hey. Wait a minute. You *are* in heaven. Open your eyes and look around. See! You *are* in heaven."

Life is a bunch of layers. You can lift them, one by one, and see the only layer that doesn't change.

Otherwise, all you have is you and a whole bunch of zeros. And you're trying to figure out

And this heaven is more heavenly than the heaven of ideas. Not constant temperature. That doesn't mean anything. And angels on their harp—how many? There better be only one at a time, or otherwise they all need to be playing the same song. And wings? Well, they are in heaven, so where are they going? And feathers everywhere!

And then the whole concept of hell, only to promote heaven—to scare you into wanting to go to heaven. Just that. To scare you. Let me tell you, there is a hell here, now. This hell is worse than the imagined hell.

And there is a heaven—on earth, here, now. And in this heaven, yes, there is music. But the music plays within you. It is the loveliest, loveliest *twang* of the breath, and the instrument is not being played by you. This instrument is being played by *the* player. With every strum you get what? You get life. One more moment where you can think, you can feel, you can understand, you can have clarity. These are the possibilities.

Peace for just one day is not richness. But peace in abundance, every single day, every moment: *that* is being rich. If you want to be rich, if you want a hedge against poverty, then understand your richness, understand what you have been given. Understand what this life is about. It is not going to repeat itself.

PAST LIFETIMES
Some people have so many explanations. "You were a cow in your last lifetime. You were a bull in your last lifetime. You were an elephant in your last lifetime."

None of this can be verified, so I have to take their word for it. And their credentials are not a certificate signed by the Lord himself. The saffron robe and shaved hair are their credentials.

Somebody came to me once and said, "You were an emperor in your last lifetime." Great for stroking the ego. For a moment, I felt like, "Wow. I'm important. I was an emperor!"

Just because you had breakfast doesn't mean you don't need to have dinner, right? You slept last night. Why do you want to sleep tonight again? "In my last lifetime, I was this." "In my last lifetime, I was that." "I was doing this, I was doing that." What has that got to do with *this* lifetime? Does that give me a license to be unconscious? If I don't understand the value of what is present in my life—not absent, present!—I will live in the grandest illusion there is. Because I don't know.

LIGHT
I travel a lot, and stay at different places. One day I got up in the middle of the night. I wanted to go to the bathroom, and I ended up going completely in the wrong direction—and there was no door there! I'm standing by the wall, and in the dark I'm searching for the door. And I'm computing in my head, "Did somebody move the door? Why can't I find the door?" Finally I went back to the bed, found a flashlight, turned it on. And said, "Okay. Embarrassing, but it's all right. That's the door I'm looking for."

All the reasons in the world are not going to be able to explain the situation. If there is no light in my

life, I can speculate in the darkness. But reality will not change because of my speculation.

You are faced with many things that are nothing but lies. And what are they? The illusion. What illusion? A wall in which there is no door. If I am looking for a door that doesn't exist, I will never find it.

I need light to be able to see clearly what is where. I don't need something that changes the room. There is a big difference. If you're looking for a light that creates the road, it's an illusion. Light should do one thing and one thing only: illuminate what is there. I have enough sense in me to find the road. All I need is to be able to see it.

That's the light you want in your life. That's the clarity you need in your life. Not something that creates pseudo realities, but the clarity that illuminates the reality so you can see. You can see the obstacles, and you can see the clear path, and then you can choose.

A light that creates the road is an illusion. Light should only do one thing: illuminate what is already there.

CHOICE

You want to be in clarity? That is your choice. You want peace in your life? That is your choice. And it *always* should be your choice.

Nobody should come to you and say, "If you don't do this, that's it. You're toast." No. Peace is not a realm of threats. Peace is a realm of choice. Clarity is a realm of choice, not tests: "Let's see if you'll survive this!" No. Choice!

You can choose an enjoyment and acceptance of that breath, acceptance of that richness, acceptance of what you are being given, so you can be rich.

And then, when you become rich, what do you do? Should you share your wealth? Good one. How do you share your breath? Can't do it.

I have just become incredibly rich because I have discovered the abundance and the preciousness of the breath. And what should I do with it? Enjoy it! Otherwise, what's the point of being rich?

The point is to dance, to feel the gratitude in your heart of hearts; this is enjoyment at its best. To feel alive and to be thankful for feeling alive. To feel: "Ah! I'm alive today." Do *I* have problems? Yes, I have problems. Will they go away? I hope so. Also I know hoping them away isn't going to get them to go away. Hoping them away is like inviting more. You have to do something about it. You have to put up a fence.

REALITY
The reality is that I am alive. And I need to feel grateful for this richness that I have been given. Abundance? Yes. But not forever. While I am here, it is abundant, day and night. No Sundays off. No Mondays off. No Tuesdays off. No Wednesdays off. No holidays off.

That's the blessing. It's unique. Is it precious? Of course. When you understand this, you say, "Thank you! Thank you for letting me *see* the preciousness. That's what made me rich. It was happening before, but I didn't recognize it." Recognition. Recognition of what you have been given. Recognition of this life. Recognition of being alive. This is how you celebrate.

Celebrate in gratitude. Celebrate in the most simple way. Breath isn't the only gift that you have been given. There is another gift, and another gift, and another gift that makes you rich. And you need to understand the richness of all of that. Peace has also been placed inside of you. And not only is it precious, but there is an abundance of it; to last for the rest of your life.

As if that isn't enough, you have also been blessed with love. You have also been blessed with the ability to look, to see—called *admiration*. Do you realize these are incredibly powerful gifts? Scientists can explain why a sunset is a certain color, but not why we enjoy it. What's the science behind enjoying a sunset, or enjoying a star? Enjoying a cloud? Enjoying a wave?

GOOD COMPANY
Oh, there is a science. It is the science of the heart. It is when we feel part of this magnificent drama called *existence*. It's a drama; it's a play. The director, the writer, the composer is that incredible power. It's the best show in town. You should watch it. I think you will enjoy it. The direction is magnificent.

The acting needs a lot of improvement. But, being in the company of good actors, as they say, something might rub off on you. So you can see the simplicity in your life. So you can feel the gratitude. Feel—not know, but *feel* rich. Not just know that you are blessed, but *feel* blessed.

Economically speaking, these are very hard times for many people—and not just in one country, but all over the world. And this is the conversation:

"The economy, the economy, the economy, the economy."

But I have a question for you. How about *your* economy? How about *your* prosperity? Shouldn't you be prosperous when you are so rich, when you have been given the gift of something that is incredibly precious and in abundance? But do you know?

Find that reality in your life and experience it. Stand on reality. Not on imagination, not on ideas and philosophies and ideology. This is about *you* feeling that reality. It's about *you* enjoying your existence because you recognize how rich you are. You are rich! Play. Sing. Play something wonderful for yourself. Nobody else is going to hear the music that I'm talking about. It is not a performance.

SURPRISING WORLD OF MUSIC

This song you will play is only for yourself. Play well. And play with all that beautiful emotion that you can put into it. Remember the silence, remember the notes, remember the sequence, and play. Play for yourself, and enjoy every movement as it takes you into the surprising world of music within you.

Recognize the *twang* of each breath. How beautiful. Whose finger is on this string? Not mine. Someone very special. Somebody extremely special is twanging this for me. That is my blessing. I want to be silent. I want to listen. I want to enjoy. I want to be mesmerized.

And in this, I am brought back to clarity. I remember what I am about. Not the journey of a thousand miles, but just one step, one day. One day at a time. To where? To me, to my heart, to my existence.

Not to the God up in clouds, but to the God that dances in my heart. To that God that has made this house: me! I want to spend some time there. I want to know. I want to understand. I want to feel that clarity.

That's enjoyment. Incredible enjoyment—and it makes me feel so rich, so rich, so rich. And this is how it should be for you, too. You should know, and feel rich. Enjoyment because you are rich. Be fulfilled. That's the little trick to happiness. That's the little trick to peace.

Stand not on imagination, but on reality. Find that reality in your life and experience it.

THE 3 IDIOTS

WE CALL THEM IDIOTS. BUT THE REASON WE LAUGH AT THEM IS BECAUSE WE SEE A FAMILIARITY.

Once there was a king who asked his general to find him three idiots. The general was a little puzzled, but it was the king's order so he set out searching for three idiots. And he came across a lot of people, but none of them looked like idiots to him.

Finally, after searching and searching and searching, he sees a man who has fallen on the ground. His legs are moving, but his arms are fixed wide apart in the air. He tries to get up, but he can't—because his arms are in the air.

So the general goes up to the man and says, "What's the matter with you?" The man says, "First, get me up." So the general helps him up. And with his arms still spread out, the man says, "My wife is redecorating our house. And she told me to go buy a curtain this wide. And I don't want to move my hands, because if I do, the dimensions will change, and my wife will be very unhappy."

The general said, "Could you meet me in the city square tomorrow?" And he went looking for a second idiot. He's searching, searching, searching—can't find anybody. Finally, he sees a man with a big load of wood on his head, riding a donkey. So he goes up to the man. He says, "You're sitting on the donkey.

Why are you carrying this big load of wood on your head?" And the man says, "I love my donkey. He helps me so much, and he's carrying me. I didn't want my donkey to be burdened by the extra load of wood, so I'm carrying it on my head."

The general said, "Could you meet me tomorrow in the city square?" Then again, he goes looking, looking, looking, and by this time, it's already night. Then he sees a man on his hands and knees, searching around a lamppost. He walks over to the man and says, "What are you doing?" The man says, "This afternoon, I was with some friends in the jungle—and I have a bad habit. I play with my ring when I talk. So I was playing with my ring, and it fell off. And now I'm searching for it." The general said, "But if it fell in the jungle, why are you searching for it here?" The man says, "There is no light in the jungle, but there is light here. So I'm searching here."

WE ARE THE IDIOTS

There they are. And we call them idiots. We think they are funny. But the reason we laugh at them is because we see a familiarity. We can relate. In our lives, we too walk around with our arms spread out. "This is it! I'm rich. I have a great job.

I have this. I have that, and I don't want to change that." And if you fall, can you get up? No. Do you have to endure suffering? Yes. Endure pain? Yes. Are you away from peace? Yes. Still you say, "But I don't want to change this."

And you walk through your whole life like that: "This is how life is. Sometimes it's good. Sometimes it's bad. This is it."

And there's our second idiot who says, "I love my donkey, and I don't want to burden it." People say, "Everything I do is for my family. I want my family to be happy." Even though *they* are unhappy, they think somehow their enduring unhappiness is helping their family. They say, "I am carrying the load on my neck. It's not burdening the family."

This is simple ignorance. Take it one step further. People say, "Whatever I am, whatever I think, only affects me, and no one else." This is not true.

Look at the situation of the world. Every country justifies killing: "Oh, preemptive killing. They may hurt us, so let's get them first." What you do affects your family, it affects your friends, your country, your city, your house. It affects everything, even your dog, even your cat! And that's why you need not to believe, but to know.

Then there is the third idiot: "It's somewhere else, but I'm searching here because it is convenient." The divinity resides within all of us, and everybody searches for that divinity on the outside. Why? Because it is convenient!

BELIEVING OR KNOWING

Where is God? Everybody says, "God? Where? As far away as possible!" Then somebody comes along and says, "God is in you!" And people say, "In me? No way!" Why? Because it is convenient. The responsibility that it would place upon you to actually know the divinity that resides in you, you think, would be immense. "Oh my! You mean—in *me*?" But that's the truth!

Today mankind is caught in the web of belief. Everything is "Believe, believe, believe." What happened to knowing? What is the value of knowing? In believing, there is no knowing; but in knowing, believing is automatically included.

When something is important in your life, do you believe or do you want to know? It's a simple question. When a man falls in love with a woman,

is the man just supposed to believe that she will marry him? No. He asks, "Will you marry me?" And if she says, "Believe whatever you want," that means "No!"

So how can we just believe there is something called "peace" that the world needs? People say to me, "Oh, I'm so glad you are working on bringing world peace." And I say to them, "I'm not."

I have been around the world I don't even know how many times, and I can tell you one thing. The world doesn't need peace. We human beings need peace; not the crows, not the cockroaches. If somebody is making the cockroaches' life difficult, it's us. We are the ones who need peace. The peace has to be, by its very nature, in our hearts, so that we feel it every single day. Not just once: "Oh, yeah. I felt peace once, in 1922, and that was it." No. Every day you have to feel peace. And where is it? Like our third idiot, we're looking for it somewhere else.

It's a simple question: When something is important, do you believe or do you want to know?

THE FOX AND THE GRAPES

Some people believe there is no God. When a woman breaks their heart, men say, "I will never fall in love again! There is no true love!" And women say the same thing: "Oh, those men! I will never look at a man again!" They say, "This love

72

thing is overrated. There is no such thing as true love." Have you heard something like that?

Remember the story about the fox that tried to jump and jump to get to the grapes? And when the fox couldn't get to the grapes, it said, "Ugh! The grapes are sour." Same thing, same exact mentality, same exact thought process. "Nah, there can never be peace."

I want to tell you there is already peace—inside you. But I also know that you know that. And I also know that if you don't feel it, it doesn't mean anything to you. You need to know, without uncertainty. And that is what has to happen. Not ideas and philosophies, please! Reality! I want to tell you to say yes to the thirst. Not, "Nah, nah. I don't want to be thirsty." I say, "Say yes to the thirst, because it is the thirst that'll lead you to water."

NOW

Let's talk about another aspect, and for some of you it will be hot, fresh news. This moment now is the moment that you live in. Period! You do not live in the moment that just went by.

This now is where everything called existence is happening. Do you understand this now?

How happy would you be if every time you went home, you never got to your house? You got to your neighbor's, the one in front or the one in the back, but never to your own house. How happy would you be? But that is what happens in your life. You never get to the moment called now. You always go looking for the next one or the last one.

But now is where peace resides. Now is where the divinity resides. Now is where you reside. And if you're looking for it somewhere else, then welcome to the world of the third idiot, the one who was looking for his ring under the lamppost.

What is there in the now? A little *sliver* of existence moving across. No pain. No suffering. No contemplation. No memories. Nothing of the past and nothing of the future. This moment is where peace is. Peace is not in the future.

Your worries come, either when the past is reflected into the future, or when you contemplate, "What is going to happen to me?" When you are in the moment called now, you know you are okay. You are home!

If you want to find peace, peace is in your heart, with you all the time, 24/7. But only accessible in the moment called now.

I know you have learned a lot of things in your life. But you need to learn one more: how to live in this moment now.

> When you are in the moment called now, you know you are okay. You are home!

73

NO ORDINARY BOX

THERE ARE MORE THAN SEVEN BILLION BOXES ON THIS EARTH. SO WHAT IS THE VALUE OF SUCH A BOX?

There is a simple box. It has a priceless diamond inside. If you don't know about the diamond, you might treat it like any other box: you will look at it, observe the color and the size, and say, "Nothing special. There are a lot of boxes like this."

But if you knew that a very precious diamond was inside this box, all of a sudden it is no ordinary box. It's very precious. And it will be handled with that in mind.

For all of us, our body is a box. And there are more than seven billion boxes on this earth. So what is the value of such a box?

Two days ago was my daughter's birthday. I went to a large department store to get her a present. I walk in, and there are all these people. And they can see me as I can see them, but they don't say, "Hello" or anything. They want to go where they want to go, and I just want to go where I want to go. Because we are just boxes: a box from Madrid, a box from Barcelona. You see a box wearing a sari: "That's a box from India." You see somebody with half cut-off jeans, baggy pants, strange shoes: "That's a box from America." And young boxes, old boxes. Once in a while, "That's a nicer box," or, "It was a nice box." And this is how it is for us every day.

THE CONTENT

I want to talk about the contents of the "human box," and then you decide if the contents of this box could make it precious.

The content that has been placed in this human box is the divine. What is the divine? The divine is the beauty that was, is, and will be. It is the power that sustains the entire creation; that from dust creates amazing things, and brings them back to dust again. To call it powerful, even to call it all powerful, would be underestimating its power, because its power is such that no human mind can even begin to comprehend it.

Sometimes we go to a restaurant and somebody asks how our meal was, and we say, "Oh, it was out of this world." Now, in my book, there are only a handful of people—the astronauts—who can actually say, "It's out of this world." And what did they eat out there? It wasn't fresh. But people say things like, "Out of this world." "Oh, it was unimaginable."

Scriptures that were written thousands of years ago say that only the divine is unimaginable. Everything else can be imagined. And that divine is within you.

Being alive, bound by time, is called *existence*. I exist. You exist. But the question is: Do we know about the divinity residing in this box? The word is knowing—not believing—*knowing*. How do you know? How do you know anything? You have to be conscious to know, and you have to be unconscious to not know.

This human body is a box, and in this box is the divine—not Santa Claus. Big difference, Santa fulfills little children's wishes. The divine does not fall into that realm. Yet so many of us look at the divine as Santa Claus. Santa is not divine. Why? Santa has to come and go. The divine is the only one that cannot come and go. How can it? Where is the divine going to come from? It's everywhere. Where is it going to go? Nowhere. It has nowhere to go.

So that is the divine. Our existence is being here, bound by time. We exist. And now there is the possibility of two things: knowing and not knowing. Not knowing? This box will be just another box in the midst of all the boxes that are here. Knowing will make all the difference in the care, the handling, the value, and the respect that this box would be due. Not because of itself, but because of what is *in* it.

THINKING, THINKING, THINKING

Not knowing brings you doubt. Doubt brings you anxiety. Knowing brings you peace. Peace is

not on top of a mountain. Absolutely not! Some people think so. The word is *think!* Does this box think? Oh, yes. This box thinks and thinks and thinks. One day this box thinks, "I am so great!" One day the box thinks, "I'm not so great." One day the box thinks, "I am on top of the world." One day the box thinks, "The world is on top of me." One day the box thinks, "Everything is going my way." One day the box thinks, "I am going everyone else's way. No one is going my way."

But why does this box think so much? You look at some people, you look at their faces, then you look at how they look at you. A smile is good. A serious face is not good. And a face turned away? Very bad. And the box even likes to know what other boxes are thinking. Saturation of thinking. And the box wants to know, "What are you thinking?" And the box gets very fascinated when somebody says, "I know what you are thinking." The box says, "Wow! You know what I am thinking. You must be enlightened."

The value of this box can only be measured by knowing what's in it.

Everyone is thinking and thinking and thinking. We go to the doctor, and the doctor says, "Do you know what I am thinking?" And all we can say is, "I hope you are not thinking what I am thinking." When the policeman pulls you over, he says, "You were speeding." And you say, "You know what I was thinking? Maybe this time you will let me go." It is the game of thinking.

And for our dear one? Beautiful restaurant, beautiful meal. Hold the beloved's hand. This is before marriage. Hold the hand, and then you say, "So, what are you thinking?" We're thinking and we're thinking and we're thinking. And our world leaders stand behind the microphone, tall. And they say, "Do you know what I am thinking?" And to them we say, "I hope you are thinking the same thing I am thinking."

And when you order your meal in a restaurant, and the waiter says, "Do you know what I was thinking?" you say, "I don't want to know what you were thinking. Just bring me what I ordered."

So here we are, surrounded with thinking, thinking, thinking. What could make that process of thinking fairly redundant? Knowing! When you know, you don't have to think because you know. But because we don't know, we think and we think, till we're blue in the face—literally, dead in the coffin—blue in the face. And somebody comes over and says, "Do you know what I was thinking?" You don't. This box doesn't always let on what it is thinking.

HONORING EXISTENCE

I talk about knowing. That doesn't mean you have to stop thinking. But when you know, you have the luxury of thinking about what you want to think about. Because the ability to think is God's gift to you; and what you think about is your gift to yourself. But if you do not know, you are caught in the grind of doubt, and nothing seems to work for you. You say, "I make the effort. Where is this going? Where will this end?" The answer is in the knowing that the most incredible of all that could be accomplished has been accomplished. You are alive!

So what do you think? What do you know? Are you alive, truly knowing that the divine is within you? If yes, you would be the box that would say, "I will do everything to honor that diamond that is within me and be as flawless as I can be. No dirt, no smudge. As clean as I can be, as shiny as I can be, as much in peace as I can be."

This is when you honor the divine. Not a placard on the wall. Not a sentence, not a prayer, not a word. Not a verb, not a noun, not a proverb, not an adverb, but the real honoring of existence.

Now I know that through thought you fight the very words I speak. And yet, in your heart you have no problem with it. It understands. And it finds it not new, or unique, or impossible, but it delights—not in thought, but in knowing. The response from the heart is: "So it is!" But your head says, "Let me think about it."

There is much to be learned from books, there is much to be learned from science, there is much to be learned in the world. Much. And there is much to be learned from understanding. There is much to be learned from knowing the contents of this box. Because on one hand, what I speak about is so amazingly simple—because

it's already there. I mean, I am not talking about how we are going to fly the divine into you. The divine is already there.

For some people, this box is the reality; and for some people, what's in the box is the reality. They honor this box, not because of the box. How many people honor this box because of the box, because of the way the box looks? And when the box doesn't look so good anymore? "Ugh!" But the box *will* change. That's the nature of the box. Every day you are changing.

CHANGE

That change is starting as subtly as your hair coming out every day. Even if you have a whole head full of hair, one falls off; another falls off. Skin sloughing off, cells being regenerated, cells dying. On an incredibly small level, you are constantly changing. You hate that. You hate the inevitable.

A lot of young people think, "I've been waiting for change for the last ten years. I don't have a beard yet," and this and that. Patience. It's coming big time. And then the war begins, but never the recognition, never understanding that the value of this box can only be measured by the recognition of its contents, by knowing that which is inside the box.

To me, this is so simple. It is all you have to know, and it can change the entire equation. When you know, then the truest excitement for being alive starts to happen. You become aware. Not about the passage of time, but about the value of existence. Because remember what existence is; it is being alive bracketed by time.

Do we all eat the same food? No. Do we live in the same house? No. Do we like the same colors? No. Do we like the same music? Absolutely not. Do we look the same? Absolutely not. Our preferences are completely different. Some people when they go to sleep lie on their backs. Some people lie on the left side, some people lie on the right side. Some people lie upside-down. Some people walk in their sleep. Some people talk in their sleep. Some people can't sleep. So, are we all different? The world says we are.

BREATH

I say that one day you came in this world and there was something that needed to happen. And if it didn't happen, the doctor was very persistent that it should happen. So was everybody else, very persistent. And do you know what it was? Some people think, "Oh, yeah, the name." Others think, "Find out the sex." No. It wasn't that. It was only one thing: Breathing or not?

You could've come out of your mother's womb so completely formed you already had a trimmed moustache, a nice three-piece suit, cufflinks, nice shirt, tie—perfectly groomed hair. But if you were not breathing and never got around to breathing, you were not coming home with your parents. You were going somewhere else.

Breathing or not? That's how it begins for every single person on the face of this earth—king, queen, pauper, beggar, politician, schoolteacher, unemployed. In fact, everybody is unemployed at that point. But that is not what I'm talking about. I'm talking about that it begins with the breath. And don't you find it fascinating where it ends? Not when you run out of money, not when you run out of food, not when you run out of water. This is how it happens. Even if you are hooked up to all the machines, and the machines are saying you're dead, and you're still breathing; the doctor isn't going to say you're faulty. The doctor is going to say the machine is faulty. Because you're still breathing, you're not dead. You're still alive.

It begins with your breath; it ends with your breath. You should know that, because the coming and going of the breath also has something to do with the divine. Your existence has something to do with the divine. Life is about the joy that you need to experience. It is about the peace that should be dancing all around you. There should be contentment, there should be a reality. And you should have available to you a resource that can connect you back to that knowing if ever you get disconnected from it and start thinking about the knowing. That's insurance.

This is about standing on your own feet. This is about *you* knowing. Not about hearsay. Not about, "I read that in a book." No. It's about you knowing yourself.

RECOGNITION

I want to know. I want to be free from doubt as much as possible in my existence. I know I was born and that one day I have to go. I know what is going to happen to me. A lot of people don't understand this. Now many societies are getting into recycling, but the divine came up with the idea of recycling a long time ago. On this planet earth very little new stuff comes down. Whatever is around here is recycled, everything gets recycled. This box will get recycled, too.

this earth, makes you really special. It's not your ideas. Thoughts change. They will. New discoveries will come, of course. But this is not what makes you special. When you honor that peace, that's what makes you special. When you recognize the divine in you, that's what makes you special. Even if this recognition in your busy lifetime is for one hour, five minutes, ten minutes or for one second. That recognition is what makes you special, that you recognize that you are no ordinary box.

It begins with your breath.
It ends with your breath.
You should know that.

The issue is knowing, because that is the only thing that, for this limited time that you have on

Enjoy this life. Honor the peace. Shine. As long as you are alive, as long as you exist, the divine is occupying this box. And that is not an ordinary thing. Can you imagine if every human being understood this? Even for one minute? If they could let their heart rule and understand and recognize the preciousness of this box, this world would change. And I don't think so, I *know* it. Because I have seen that remarkable change in people's lives.

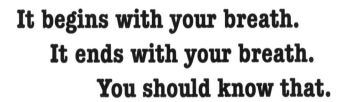

As long as you live, the divine is occupying this box. And that is not an ordinary thing.

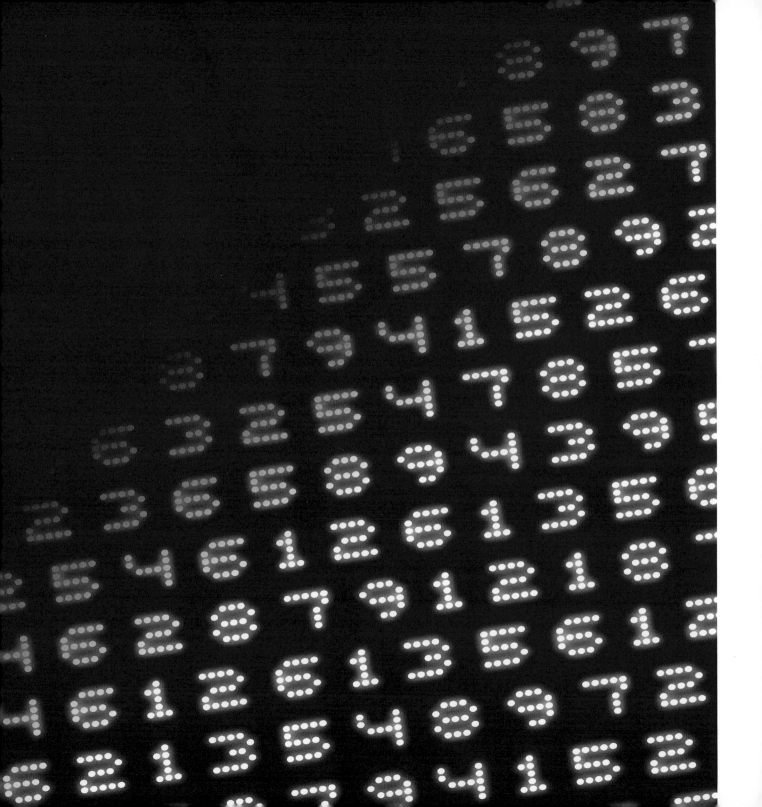

PART THREE

THE FACTS

Will this earth be gone one day?
Fact or fiction? Fact: it'll be gone.

Will the sun be gone?
Fact or fiction? It'll be gone.

Should you know yourself?
Fact or fiction? Fact!

DON'T BELIEVE ME

THE INFINITE IN YOU IS REAL. KNOW IT. DON'T JUST BELIEVE IN IT.

It's a common scientific understanding that everything that has been created will one day be destroyed. Now you get up in the morning, you pick up your newspaper. You get a cup of coffee, you sit down at the table, and you relax. And you're starting your day. Do you really have that thought in your mind that everything that has been created will be destroyed? No!

I AM DYING

At night you look up and see the stars and the moon. Does that fall into the category of something that was created? Yes. Not only the sun, not only the moon, not only the earth, but the entire universe, and all the universes that we don't even know about, are destined to be destroyed. So I ask, who are you?

You think you know who you are. Your husband sees you: "Oh, that's my wife." Your child sees you: "That's my mother." Your sister sees you: "That's my sister." Is that who we are?

I had a Skype call. Somebody told me, "There is somebody who wants to talk to you. This person is dying." So the day came. And when I got up,

I knew there was going to be this call. Immediately I thought about it. "What are you going to tell a person who's dying?" They know they're dying. They are feeling pain, they're feeling weak. It's happening.

Having my coffee, I'm thinking, I'm thinking, I'm thinking. "Bing!" Everybody is dying! I am dying! Say that which you would say to everyone. These elements that we are made of? That's the mother. That's the father. That's the great cook. That's the great artist, the great writer. These elements stay here. They are all being recycled. Dust goes back to being dust. And there is something of the infinite in you. That remains infinite forever. Because it is the only thing that was never created, and it will never be destroyed.

THE RIVER

Other people introduce you to the elements. I introduce you to the infinite in you. And I say, "That is real. The other stuff is not." Do you know, do you understand the reality?

Just now a drop of rain fell. In India, in South America, in North America, in Japan, in Hawaii, in Australia, in Africa. One drop fell, and another one fell, and another, and another, and another. And as a consequence, it gave birth to the mighty rivers in each of the continents. One drop, followed by another, another, another, another, gave birth to the Amazon. Gave birth to the Ganges. Gave birth to the mighty Colorado. To the Rhine.

When the great river flows, it brings water to the parched areas. It makes journeys possible. It

makes food possible. It provides the fertile grounds for the birds to come and sit. It takes the fertile soil to the places where it is needed. And all rivers ultimately join the ocean from where they came.

But here is another river. A moment in time came and left, came and left, came and left. These moments give birth to a river called life. Now this river of life that is yours, what does it do? Does it have opinions? Ideas?

There is that famous painting of God holding out his finger toward the man. I was looking at it the

WHY ME?

People are killing each other. Why? Do we respect each other? No! Why don't we respect each other? Because to respect another person, first you have to respect yourself. If you don't respect yourself, you cannot respect another person. Do you respect yourself? No!

There was a man who was totally into God. Every day he would pray, pray, pray. He did everything he was asked by his religion. And one day he realized that his neighbor does not believe in God. He is an atheist. And he has a great job, great wife, beautiful house, beautiful kids. And this man has, like, nothing!

So one day he's deep into his prayer, and he says, "Lord, I love you so much. I believe in you. From morning till evening I pray and I pray and I pray and I pray. And I have nothing! My wife, she's hardly ever home. My children, they don't listen to me. And my neighbor? Gorgeous wife. She's home, cooks for him, takes care of the house. The house is incredible. His children are amazing. Why? Why is this?"

All of a sudden there was this voice from the heaven: *Boomf!* "Because he doesn't bother me all day long!"

It's funny. Why is it funny? Because that's too human. God should be slightly human. Not *too* human.

We need to understand one thing: that divinity has a level of generosity that is unparalleled; has given and given and given and given! Given you

other day, and I wondered if God's really saying, "Watch it. You're going to screw everything up!" Because that's what is happening right now. The world has become "Me-me-me-me, me-me-me-me, me-me-me-me." Not a river anymore!

The world has become "Me-me-me, me-me-me."

Not a river anymore!

the most amazing planet Earth. Given you the moon. Given you the ability to see the stars. Given you the ability to feel joy. Given you the ability to feel happiness. Given you the gift of breath, again and again and again and again.

This is generosity unparalleled. Do you see it? Do you see it that way? Do you understand what that means? One day this river of life will stop flowing. But as long as it flows, it must manifest its potential, its reality, its beauty, its joy, its clarity, its understanding, its gratitude, its oneness. And it needs to be real for you every single day. Not one day, not one hour, but every single day. You need to be in that passion, in that love that comes not from the head, but from the heart.

HEAD OR HEART?

Why not from the head? And why from the heart? Because this head cannot tell the difference between real and fake. It is fooled all the time. You are at the airport. You are waiting for a taxi. You have got your luggage. Somebody comes along, drops a little money and says to you, "Is that yours?" The head sees the money, you go to pick it up. The thief takes the bag, and is gone. This head doesn't know. Oh, it pretends to be the knower. But it doesn't know.

If this head knew, you think there would ever be a divorce? They say, "Oh, I love you!" "I love you!" The minister says, "Do you take this person to be your lawfully wedded husband" (or "wife"), "till death do you part?" And what does this head do? With a little tear and a little quivering of the lips: "I do!" Six months later? "Get out of my house!" What happened to that little tear? What

happened to the quivering lips? What happened to "our love"? *Whoosh!* And this head does that all the time. Go home and open your closet and see if there is anything there you don't wear any more. And if you find there is, the reason is, this head said, "Oh, you would look so good in that!" Now it says, "Naah."

The whole world is dancing a dance of the head. It's okay. It's not a problem. As long as you know the difference between the head and the heart. The heart does not get deceived. The head refers to the heart, "Oh, this is from the bottom of my heart." But the heart never says, "Oh, this is from the bottom of my head." Never!

To your mind, you are important. And because you are important, you have a license to be rude, to be unkind to other people. In the realm of heart, there is no reason to be rude or unkind to anyone. The mind sees the differences. The heart sees the similarity. "You are alive. I am alive. You are a human being. I am a human being."

LISTEN

We have two ears, and we don't even use one. We have two! And they're always open. But we close them. We don't listen to each other. Try this: the day you want to make a little heaven for your kid or your spouse, or any other person, just listen to them. And the day you want to make a heaven for yourself, just listen to your heart. You will not hear a long list of wishes, but just a call to be fulfilled. To be in real joy. To have savored, to have known the divine, because it was so close to you. To you! Not out there. But here, in you. Then, that day you will be free. Free!

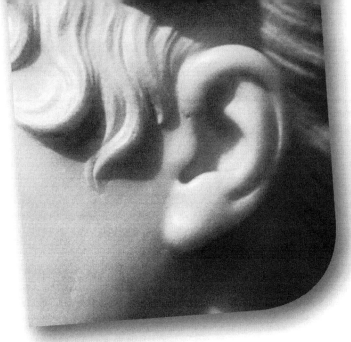

The day you listen to your heart, you will not hear a long list, just a call to be fulfilled. To be in real joy.

And so I find it curious that you do not know how to respect yourself. Something is wrong. And I know what is wrong. You are only looking at the vessel, not at what's in it. The day you have a recognition of what is in it will be the day that even the *idea* of peace will begin to make sense.

That day you will dance with the divine. That day you will understand what reality is. That day you will understand what truth is. That is the day you will understand what respect is. That is the day you will become a human being.

A VESSEL

This human body is a vessel. And what is its value? Well, it depends. What's in it? The divine. What is the value of divine? What is it? It is by the courtesy of that divine that all the gold in this universe and the universes beyond exists. It is by the courtesy of the divine that every drop of water, every atom of oxygen, every molecule of hydrogen exists.

It is by the courtesy of that infinite that anything exists. The value of that divinity is beyond any concept that anybody could ever have. So how precious are you? Unfathomable. As long as the divine is in you, it's unfathomable. When the divine is gone? Nothing.

LEARN TO DANCE

You say to people, "Peace." And they say, "What peace? How can there be peace?" What choice do we have? If what is happening in the world today keeps happening , the human race is not going to be around. It is self-destructive. Why is one person killing another person that they don't even know? They're standing far away. They have been given a gun. They point the gun, they look through the little scope. And they say, "I got one!" *Pow!* And the person is dead.

Are these the signs of intelligent people? Excuse me, no! In the old days, it was great. The king himself used to fight. They have to bring that tradition back: If the countries' leaders want war, they have to be the first ones to go into battle. Then you will see a change! "Uh oh! No! Wait!" Everybody will become very saintly: "We shouldn't really be fighting with each other. Let's talk."

Why can't you talk to another person? They won't listen. And this is why it is so important in your life to know that divinity. Because you're surrounded by it. Below you, above you, in you, outside of you is the beautiful dance of this divinity. Either learn to dance with that dance or, one day, the river is going to stop flowing.

What's bad about the river stopping? Nothing, except for one thing. Now you cannot do what you could have done when you were alive. You do so much so you can be alive. You work so you can eat. You have a house or apartment so you can live. And yet you don't understand what it means to be alive. And then, what's the point?

THE WORLD IS NOT THE PROBLEM
This world is in the same situation as the donkey that goes around the well. They use this quite a bit in India and some of the Middle Eastern countries. An ox or a donkey goes around the well, hooked up through the gears to some small buckets. It goes around and around and around the well all day long, turning the wheels. And to prevent it from becoming distracted, so it will keep going around and around, they blindfold it. And I'm sure the donkey is wondering, "Man, I have come a long ways. Surely I have escaped." As soon as the blindfold comes off: "Uh-oh. I'm still in the same place."

You think the situation of the world is like that? "Oh, education! Once we are educated, the world will be a better place." I'm not against education, but there are more schools now than there ever were. There are more universities now than there ever were. And there is the great "World Wide Web"—more information than there ever was. There are more books now than there ever were. And there are more wars than there ever were.

People say, "You talk about divinity, you talk about life. But there are people hungry out there!" You want to hear a statistic? Fifty percent of the world's food supply is wasted! So let's see. There are people who are hungry, and fifty percent of the food is wasted. Hmm. Who should we blame for this? "Ah! Let's blame God!" How convenient.

You work so you can eat, so you can have a place where you can live.

And yet you don't understand what it means to be alive.

So how smart are we? You like technology? It cannot save fifty percent of the food. We are not the divine, and we should stop pretending to be. We are human beings, the containers of the divine. Time has come for us to understand ourselves. As Socrates said a long time ago, "Know thyself." And we still haven't done it. The time has come to do that. The time has come to understand the divine within us.

The world is not the problem. We are. Earth makes more than enough food for everybody. But we all have a magic wand, and our magic wand is not very nice. It's the wand of greed.

Whatever it touches, it destroys. The time has come for the fairy godmother to put away the wand for a little while and start doing things with consciousness, with understanding; understanding of the self.

DON'T BELIEVE ME

Begin with respect for yourself, for your fellow beings, for this earth. It all begins from you. You are the drop, the source of that river. You are the container of divinity. You are so incredibly fortunate. Now *know* it. Don't believe it; know it. This is why I say, "Don't believe me." Not too many people can say that.

If the politicians started saying, "Don't believe me," they would be in trouble. If the religious orders started saying, "Don't believe us," they would be in trouble. Me, I'm not a believer. I want to know. And you should know, too. So I can say, "Don't believe me. *Know* what I know. And then you will know what I am talking about."

I really, really wish you didn't believe a word I say. And instead you said, "I've got to know!" And if you became like that in your life: "I've got to know!", you would be so filled with peace. But don't believe that. Know it for yourself.

> If you became like that: "I've got to know!"
> you would be filled with peace.
> But don't believe this.
> Know it for yourself.

THE CURE IS CONSCIOUSNESS

THERE IS A DEADLY DISEASE, AND ONCE YOU GET IT, IT'S REALLY HARD TO KICK.

When you get to the end of your road—nowhere to go, and things look pretty hopeless—turn around. Because that's the beginning of another road. And that's how existence has to be. It has to be fulfilling. Every day has to be as beautiful as it can be, because it doesn't come back.

Does that make it precious for you? Does that make it real for you? Do you understand the dynamics of a single day? Do you understand the dynamics of one lifetime? Do you understand the dynamics of every breath? Do you understand the dynamics of existence?

In this drama of ours, we are in the middle of two forces pulling on us. You have to learn the art—and it is an art—of which one to resist and which one to allow yourself to be pulled by. And you have to know the difference, and you have to know what you're doing. When clarity pulls on you, do not resist. Just let go. Let it pull you. When frustration tugs on you, resist.

How come we're not, all of us, experts at this? It's because of the most pervasive human disease. There are a lot of doctors in the world, and they will not qualify this as a disease, but it is. And it is eating away at humanity. And not one country, island, cave, nook, cranny, avenue, street, or building is exempt from it.

It's a deadly disease. Once you get it, it's really hard to kick. It's called "unconsciousness."

All I am trying to do is draw your attention to certain things that you usually don't pay attention to, even though you know about them: things like clarity, like understanding, like simplicity, like fulfillment, like the heart.

LIMPING ALONG

You know about these things, but you don't always acknowledge them. Many of us at some time or the other have had a sprained ankle, causing us to hobble along.

Does that sound like the way we walk on the path of life? Absolutely. Limping along. Everyone.

We have more information available to us now than we ever did, thanks to the "WWW," the worldwide web. "Web" is the key word here—it's a web! We have so many wars, so many hungry people, so many ignored people on the face of this earth. Yet we have more educated people now than we ever did. Ever. I mean, you don't even have to have an affinity toward education these days. It'll just fall into your head. Just open your mouth.

So what is peace? Believe me, if you want to get to peace, you've got to cure the disease of unconsciousness. And there's only one cure for this disease: consciousness.

You can have peace in your life. Why? How? Because peace is in you. Nobody has to bring peace to you. You have consciousness in you, and you have unconsciousness in you. You have hate in you, you have love in you. You have clarity in you, you have confusion in you. Talk about everything. Right there, you cover it. The mortal is in you, and the immortal is in you. What you need is not some words on a piece of paper. You need a mirror to understand what is happening, to turn within and, in the quietness of your own self, listen. Not to words, but to a feeling, wanting to appreciate the feeling of being alive.

WHAT DO YOU PRACTICE?

Have you ever given a chance to those things that are good within you; those things that seek out clarity? And have you become happy at the thought of having clarity, and become elated at the presence of clarity? Of course you have. But is that what you nurture most in your life?

Whatever you practice a lot, you will get good at. Question: What do you practice? What are you good at? I know one thing we practice every single day is unconsciousness.

I thought of a word, and I looked up its meaning. It's an interesting word. It's a very common word: "restless." What exactly does it mean? We all get restless. You know what it means? It means exactly that: "rest less." No rest.

So why are you restless, when within you is the resort of resorts? Within you is the most comfortable place you can ever experience. In this beautiful ocean that resides within you, you can come and rest.

I was watching a TV show called "Wish You Were Here." The reporters go out to really beautiful places like a beautiful beach with crystal-clear water, and they report back, basically saying, "Wish you were here." The idea is to entice people to take vacations.

I can tell you one thing, every person who has been within has called out to the entire humanity and said, "Wish you were here." Because there is no place like home. And that's your home. And because it is the reality, it works. A human being is a human being, and as long as there is a human being, within them is this most precious thing.

There are people who are very afraid. They think, "If I was to go inside, what would I find?" Well, don't you hope it's good stuff? It's inside of you! What do you want to find inside of you? Horrible stuff?

WISH YOU WERE HERE

Inside of you is the most comfortable. As this body of yours is mortal, within you is the immortal. As the world can be confusing, within is clear. Every day, it's a drama. I mean, who needs to watch a movie? Just look out there. There is love. There is hate. There is suspense, there is adventure. There's mystery.

Inside you is a constant, unchanging reality. That's where you need to go.

Without it, without recognizing our immortality, all we are left with is mortality. And everybody hates it. A person goes into the doctor's office for a checkup: "Am I okay?" And the doctor says, "You know, uh . . . Yeah, you're going to . . . You have only six months to live." And then the person goes through this whole thing. "Oh, this can't be, this can't be, this can't be." Then they accept it. And I've seen them. They become bubbly. Bubbly. Appreciating every day that they get *after* the six months, because the doctor was wrong!

93

Do you understand the dynamics of a single day? Of one lifetime? Of every breath? Of existence?

But why does it have to be dire straits before clarity kicks in? Can't we have it kick in before the dire straits? And you know what that process is called? Being conscious. You have heard many people say, "Today is really important." Why?

Somebody had a sign on his refrigerator with the word "Smile." I said, "That's horrible!" And he said, "What's so horrible about that? It's great! People will look at it and smile." And I said, "If that is why they will smile, that's horrible."

You should smile because something inside you makes you smile. People pray to God, "God, please make my crops grow better." "God, I've had a Mercedes. I need to move on to the Rolls." These days, everybody just shoots out a prayer. "We're about to begin the football game. Let's pray." "We're going to blow up all known civilization. Let's pray!"

PRAYING AND WONDERING
And that's it. Pray, pray, pray, pray, pray. You want to pray? Great. But what should your prayer be like, the Santa Claus wish list? "I've been a good boy. Can I have my teddy girl?" "I've been a good girl, can I have my promotion?" Or should the prayer—I mean, excuse me, but shouldn't the prayer be,

"Thank you for this life; thank you for this breath; thank you for today; thank you for this moment"?

But it isn't. And it isn't because there is no experience of today. None. You wake up, "Ah, it's Sunday. I can sleep in." What is the experience of the moment? "What time is it? Oh, yeah, let me look at my watch."

People look at the time and don't understand the value of it. What is it telling you? It's telling you, "You're not going to be here forever."

There are people who love to question. Questioning is good. But find the answer, too! Without finding the answer, what good is it to question? "I wonder. I wonder, I wonder, I wonder." That's what people do. Wonder. And they wonder, and they wonder, "Is there really a God?" And some say, "Oh, definitely. You shouldn't be wondering if there is a God." And other people say, "No, there isn't a God." And some people say, "Well, if there is a God, how come all these crazy things are happening?"

And some people wonder what they were in their last lifetime. And there are people who say, "Don't wonder what you were in your last lifetime. I can tell you. You were an elephant!"

And the whole world wonders and wonders and wonders. And no answers. No answers.

So where are the answers? Since the questions came from within you, guess where the answers are? Within you. Within you is the vacation spot of the entire known universe.

94

And then there are people who wonder if there are aliens. Well, maybe there are aliens out there, maybe there are not aliens out there. What difference does it make to you?

You are not here courtesy of the aliens. You are here courtesy of the breath. I can almost hear people thinking, "No, no, no. Scientifically, maybe the first little amoebas and bacteria were aliens that came from out there!"

Maybe they *were*. But you are still alive courtesy of the breath. Don't you understand how simple it is? When you were born that's what the doctor was looking for: are you breathing or not? And when you go away from this world, the last form of verification will be: has he or she stopped breathing?

With breath it begins. With breath it ends. And it is one thing you will practice every day. And how come you don't understand the value of it? You should. You should understand that it is the blessing of all blessings. There are people who say, "Oh, this-and-that person is so blessed." Are you breathing? If you are, you're blessed. You are amazingly blessed, you're incredibly blessed, and there can be no greater blessing.

Maybe the first little amoebas and bacteria were aliens that came from outer space.

Maybe, but you are still alive courtesy of the breath.

A human being is full of treasures. And those treasures have to be explored and used. Consciousness has to be used. You cannot just say, "I have consciousness. I have experienced it." That's the fallacy people have about peace: You experience it one day and that's it. "Oh, yeah. I definitely have experienced peace—once. It was a long time ago when I fell in the bathtub and hit my head. I mean, it was very peaceful for a while." I mean, no! Peace has to be felt every day. Every hour, every minute, every second. The moment I am not feeling peace, something is wrong. Not right—wrong!

THE GOOD NEWS

I have just told you everything you could ever want and need to live this life to its fullest.

A lot of people say, "How do I begin?" Well, common sense would dictate that the first thing you can do is start accepting that it's all here, inside you, and quit wasting your time looking around. Because the one that you have been searching for has always been here. It's good news. It's really, really good news. A lot of people don't want good news, they want interesting news. Sorry, I don't have interesting news. Good news is all I have.

You have a gift—each living human being has a gift. Find it. And if that gift is to find the inner peace, hone it. Become good at it.

You can have peace, because peace is in you.
Hate is in you, love is in you.
Clarity is in you, confusion is in you.
The mortal is in you, the immortal is in you.

THE YOU YOU DIDN'T CHOOSE

THE PART OF US WHICH NEITHER WE NOR OUR PARENTS HAVE SHAPED IS REALLY FASCINATING.

Let's do some detective work and start with a question that's truly fascinating: Who are you? One part of the answer is very obvious. There is a part of you that your parents had a hand in shaping: which school they sent you to; how much they stood behind you and said, "Go to school! Go to school!" And then, from some point on, it was more just you. Maybe your friends had a little part in it, maybe your neighbors, maybe your girlfriend or boyfriend. But that's not the area I talk about.

I'm talking about who you are in that part of your life in which you had no control. None at all. Because the part of us which neither we nor our parents nor friends have shaped is really fascinating.

97

You were born. You had no choice in that. You came out. And when you did, you had to breathe. And if you decided to hold your breath, the doctor would hold you upside down and keep whacking you till you started breathing.

FUNDAMENTALS OF PEACE

But let's take it to another dimension, where you also didn't have a choice. Something magnificent decided to reside in you. You didn't choose that. Nobody does. There is a power that keeps me alive, that resides within me. And I never said, "Okay, you can live here." I never made any choice about it.

So, for some things, I didn't have any choice. They just were there from the moment I was born. And then there are a whole lot of other things which I choose: the colors I like, the suits I wear, the ties I wear, the music I like, the TV shows, the movies I watch.

So let's go on playing detective. Where are the fundamentals of peace? Are they in the part where I make the choices, or are they very deeply rooted in the fundamentals of me just being alive? Interesting question. Because most people think that peace is in the part where we choose. It's not. It is in the part where the roots are.

What do I mean by "roots"? Every human being is a seed. And as a seed, we have an incredible, unlimited potential. Now what does a seed need to release its potential? It needs to be placed in the environment where it can grow. If not, then it will simply remain a seed—nothing will come out of it. But plant the seed in nutritionally rich soil, water it, and its potential will manifest.

I'm not a philosopher. A philosopher would talk about the potential of the seed. I talk about the realization of that potential. I am much closer to being a gardener. I'm not telling people, "Oh, yeah, we could be like this and we could be like that. And if there is a truth, it has to live somewhere, so it must be in the pineal gland." That's interesting, very interesting. But what is the reality of a human being?

The power that keeps me alive resides within me. And I never said, "Okay. You can live here."

SADNESS

The Indian poet Kabir* likened a human being to the musk deer. The deer carries a fragrant musk in its own navel, yet searches the forest in vain for the source of that fragrance.

And this is the human condition: the sadness of not having found the source we seek.

Are human beings really sad? I see people in all the different places I travel to. They have got their phone. They are talking into it, and they're texting. They're listening to music, and they're

*Kabir lived in Northern India in the 1400s. He has become famous for his uncompromising poems that inspire people to have a direct experience of the divine within, as well as his critique of hypocrisy, caste, idolatry and empty rituals.

even dancing. Are they sad? I took a walk in a park today, and I did not see anybody crying. So why is Kabir saying that this deer is sad? What does he mean?

There is a sadness that is not necessarily expressed in tears, but it is experienced and expressed in the restlessness of a being. There is a tremendous amount of restlessness in the world. No stillness. Movement, movement, movement, every day.

A restlessness of "Where are we going?" A restlessness of "What is it all about?" A restlessness of not understanding, but acting; of thinking one thing and doing another. And this is the mistake we make: we believe that we can choose our way to peace. We can't. Because if we could, we would already have found it.

There is a sadness not expressed in tears, but in restlessness.

DIVIDING LINE

What do people call this issue of peace? "Mysterious!" There is a distinct line in your life. Certain things reside on one side and other things reside on the other side. On one side of the line, you have to know. Believing will not work. "When will the flight leave?" Do you want to believe or know? "What is in your refrigerator?" Do you want to believe or know? You open the refrigerator door, the light goes on. You look, and you say, "Ah! Now I know what's in there." And you close the door.

So on one side of the line, it all has to be knowing. But unfortunately, on the other side of the line, it's all believing. Long time ago somebody asked me, "Do you believe in God?" I was very young, just a kid. I said, "God is so important to me, I cannot afford to *believe* in God. I have to *know* God." I think he was shocked to be told this by a much younger person.

So I ask, where does the realm of peace lie? In the believing field or in the knowing field? Where does the divine lie? In the believing field or in the knowing field?

GIVEN, NOT CHOSEN

Why is this question important? Because peace is not an imagination. Life is not an imagination. The coming and going of the breath is not an imagination. It's your reality! What does it mean to you?

When the time comes to leave, and it becomes harder and harder to breathe, then it will mean everything to you. But to find out the value of the breath that late in your life is pointless. Let's do it now, while we're healthy. Because now we can take advantage of understanding those simple things.

I'm talking about the things that we were given, not those we have chosen. You were given breath. You were given existence. You were given consciousness. You were given a wonderful thing called "understanding." You were given love. You were given joy. You don't go to the supermarket and say, "I will take three packs of joy."

Now some people might say, "Well, maybe I *do* that. I go to the alcohol section and say, 'I'll take three packs of joy.'" That's not joy. That is merely to forget. I'm not talking about forgetting, but about remembering. Remembering who you are. Because you are the container that holds divinity. And you did not choose that.

Here's the issue: whatever you do the most in your life you are going to get good at. So you must be good at something. What is it?

How long does it take you to get angry? How long does it take you to become disappointed? Is disappointment what we practice in our life? Is it anger? Fear? Jealousy? If it is, then we are very good at these things.

WHAT IS PEACE?

Peace is not a state of nothing moving. This is what they show you: "a man in peace." He's sitting there with his eyes closed. But it doesn't matter how much he pretends. He knows how much the wheels of his brain are turning. *"Crunch, Crunch! Crunch, Crunch!"*—and he's thinking, "Is the person who is looking at me impressed with my demonstration of peacefulness?"

Whatever you do the most in your life you are going to get good at.

So you must be good at something. What is it?

This is what peace becomes when you live in the world of believing. Few facts remain. Facts have nothing to do with believing. Because if you could know the facts, you wouldn't have to believe.

So what are the facts? You are alive, and you are blessed by design. Not by fate, by design. You are biased toward happiness, toward contentment, toward peace, toward knowing. If you don't think you're biased toward knowing, go play with a baby.

I have a grandson, a baby boy. He wants to know, not believe. He comes to my office, and what do you think he wants to do? He wants to take his little finger and poke it into my speaker. He wants to know what that feels like.

All day long, except when he's sleeping, it's "I want to know, I want to know, I want to know." What happened to us? We were also infatuated by knowing when we were small. How did we end up such believers? What happened?

Your roots are in the most magnificent place: with the divine. If you want peace, take the seed and sow it in the fertile ground of understanding. Give it the water of knowing, of knowledge. Give it the light of clarity. Practice that which will make you more content. Not fear and anger. Practice joy. Practice clarity. Practice peace. Be thankful for what you have been given. And know that which is most important to you.

And by the way, why be in peace? Why be in clarity? Because it feels so good. It feels super good. It makes you super happy. Unbelievably grateful. Unbelievably clear. That's why we need to practice peace. And what I just told you, you already knew. How? Because this comes from the heart. It already resides within you.

You were given breath. You were given existence. You were given consciousness. You were given love. You were given joy.

HOW ARE YOU ???

BEFORE YOU CAN ANSWER THAT QUESTION, YOU NEED TO ANSWER "WHO ARE YOU?"

Is breath precious? Of course it is. It is the most precious. But we don't recognize its preciousness, because it is also the most abundant. But if you are in the hospital, dying, and you can't breathe, you're not going to say to the doctor, "What is this thing about breath?"

The point of the breath is that it brings you life. And not all the things that happen because you are alive are your life. And this is the problem. How do you know the car engine is running? When you turn it on, you hear the noise. So if you got a recording of an engine's noise and put it in your music player, could you say, "I have this car, and there is no gas required. All I need is a recording. It makes the same noise"? No! But this is what we do in our lives.

GOOD DAYS, BAD DAYS

We think, "My job, my relationships, my ideas, my responsibilities, my this, my that, all of these things are my life." And so there is a question you have been asked so many times that you answer without thinking. The question is "How are you?"

How are you? There have been good days and there have been bad days. There have been those days that you would gladly have repeated every day. And there have been those days that you do not even wish on your worst enemy.

So how are you? When I ask this question what I really ask is, "Are you in peace? Are you in joy? Are you in tranquility? Are you in serenity? Do you feel alive?" Because if you don't, something is not right. But the extent of your compromise with the issue of peace is so great that you are more than happy to say, "Some days are good, some days are bad. But you know, that's life."

Is it? I think there's another question which is not asked very frequently—and it must be asked. And I ask this question. And you need to answer this not to other people but to yourself. The question is "Who are you?"

Before you get too consumed by "How are you?" the answer to "*Who* are you?" should be abundantly clear.

JOY OR PAIN?

How do you find out who you are? It's easy to say, "Well, I'm a human being." What is a human being? "Oh, you know, I have a nose, I have two eyes, I have two ears. I have a mouth, I have a tongue, I have teeth, I have a neck, I have a head. I have a brain, inside this, somewhere."

But I say, "Are you this being that can feel joy?" If you have ever felt joy in your life, then I ask another question: "What business do you have feeling pain when you can feel joy?"

If you felt joy and you weren't sure—"Hmm. It's so ordinary." But pain? "Wow!" Suffering, crying, being depressed? "Wow!"—then you don't need to listen to what I have to say. You should look for some treatment!

But if you felt joy and you said, "I like joy. I like clarity. I like peace," then I will tell you that if this is what you want, then know that it is the most abundant. Because it is within you, within me, within all of us.

Nobody in the whole world is void of that peace, of that joy, of that happiness inside—the one that comes like a spring, bubbles from the heart of a human being. Who are you, then? You are the spring of peace. You are the residence of divinity. You are the most incredible fusion of the finite and the infinite. You are an ocean of hope. You are the most powerful being that embodies within it the human spirit. So how do you like *that* as an answer for who you are?

Nobody in the whole world is void of the joy that bubbles from the heart.

You are the spring of peace.

CLARITY

There are people who say, "But look at this world. It's crazy." Yes, a raw diamond looks just like a piece of rock, but when you bring it to an expert, the expert will hold it and say, "This is a beautiful diamond."

If you see the craziness of the world and you say, "This world is pretty crazy," that makes you an expert on craziness, doesn't it? People tell me all the time why there cannot be peace. They are the experts in *un-peace*. And I tell them, "Of course, there can be peace." Because to bring peace in your life, it is not so much that you have to do something. It is what you *don't* have to do that will make the difference.

Instead of recognizing the weakness, you have to recognize your strength. Why are you alive? Some more facts. What is this human body? It is seventy percent water, and dirt, and minerals. When was the last time you heard minerals talking?

This is why you need clarity. You look at yourself every day in the mirror, and not once do you consider yourself a miracle. You've got a problem. The miracle doesn't recognize the miracle. The blessed has forgotten what a blessing is.

Some people look at their house and say, "This is God's blessing." Then two days later it falls down. No. If you live in a nice house, that house is *your* blessing to you. But the coming and going of the breath is *God's* blessing to you. But you don't know. "Aaah. I'm busy! I have so many things to do…"

So I say it again: if you ever, ever felt joy in your life, and you're not busy feeling that joy, something is wrong.

He didn't say, "Guess who you are" or "Imagine who you are." He said, "Know who you are."

Can you imagine, you go to the airport. The airline sign is there, the counter is there. They check your baggage, they check your passport, they do everything. And then they take your ticket and they tell you, "We do everything but fly!" Is that the airline you want? No! But we do exactly the same thing. We say, "I am alive. I am this, I am that. I am so-and-so. I am this many years old. I have done this. I have been there. I have done that. And I could do this, and I could do that. But I'm not happy!"

Something is wrong. And that's why Socrates said, "Know thyself." He didn't say, "Guess who you are." He didn't say, "Imagine who you are." He said, "Know who you are." Because you are the most incredible possibility that ever will be. In your clarity, you can change. Not be a slave, but be free. Such is the power of peace! This is how it needs to be.

A musician picks up a guitar. Before starting to play, he strums to hear if anything is out of tune and, if so, to tune it. So I ask you, is

Every day you look in the mirror, and not once do you consider yourself a miracle.

You've got a problem. The miracle doesn't recognize the miracle.

Don't mistake me. I'm not putting down books. I have a lot of books. I love to read. But when I am hungry, I know when to close the book and go to the refrigerator. That's the difference most people don't know. They keep turning the pages faster and faster, and faster and faster, and faster, saying, "Why am I still hungry?"

The Indian poet Kabir said, "That there is a drop in the ocean, everyone knows. But that there is an ocean in the drop, only a few know." You are the drop. And inside you is the ocean! Do you know? Not think. Not "I *think* so." Do you *know?*

Have you found the ocean, dear drop? Because if you haven't found that ocean, then something is not right. That which is at the same time precious and abundant is slipping through your fingers. This is how we were born: empty-handed. And this is how we have to go: empty-handed. And I'm saying, "Grab that moment of joy!" People say, "My life is such a journey." Well, if you are lost, you can't really call it a journey. Going around in circles is not a journey. It's a disaster.

your guitar in tune? Because if it is not, tune it. Tune it. Tune it. Tune it. Anything else is a compromise.

BOOKS OR REALITY

I'm not talking about ideas. I'm not talking about imagination. I'm talking about knowing. What's the difference? Let's say all your life you have accumulated cookbooks, and you have a huge library: recipes from India, from America, from Australia, from France, from South America. And now you're hungry. You can't eat the books. You have to eat food. There is an absolute line between theoretical and practical.

People used to come to me when I was very, very young and they would say, "I'm searching." And I would say, "What are you searching for?" They would answer, "I'm searching for peace." And sometimes I would say, "Well, good luck, because you will need it." My point was, how can you search for something you never lost?

People say, "I'm searching for God." Good luck. You won't find God—not that way.

Where does God make his house? In the heart of all of us. Super smart. Dwell in the heart. Wherever you go, it's there. Cannot be separated. And then, when it is separated, the show is finished. The dirt now will go back to its element. It's not in its element here. Being alive is a miracle. And when that divinity is gone, when that breath is gone, then the water, the dirt, the minerals will go back to their element.

SMILE!

So this is who you are. Now you are more qualified to answer "How are you?" Next time somebody says that—"How are you?"—smile! Just think of what I just said. That should give you something to smile about. You are the ocean, in the drop. How are you? If you're in that place, with a heart full of gratitude, of clarity, of peace dancing inside of you, there are no words to describe how you are. No words!

You don't know what's going to happen tomorrow. But tomorrow, if you get up, don't think about your problems. Truly understand, without doubt, how fortunate you are. It's the little things, the way we see things, that makes the difference. We need to see ourselves through the eyes of the one who created us. Then we'll understand the value of breath. Then we will understand what peace truly is.

When your heart is full of gratitude and peace there are no words to describe how you are. If somebody says, "How are you?" just smile!

IN THE FEELING MACHINE

DON'T JUST TALK ABOUT IT. GET WITH THE FEELING. LET YOUR HEART BE FILLED WITH GRATITUDE. NOTHING ELSE IS GOOD ENOUGH.

To us humans the subject of the stars is infinitely interesting. An exploration of the heavens is infinitely interesting. Ideas about what will happen to us after we die are infinitely interesting. Egyptians got into it. Just about every culture got into it. And we've been trying to figure it all out not for a week, not for a month, not for two months, but for thousands of years. And we haven't yet figured it out.

We're talking about thousands of years of asking the same question and getting the same answer: "Don't know!" year after year, after year, after year. We humans are supposed to be the smart ones, the ones that have the ability to figure things out. Why are we failing again and again and again, for thousands of years?

Now we're not talking about Jack the baker down the street. We're not talking about the policeman who stands on the corner, or the immigration officer at the airport. We're not talking about your uncle who lives five doors down from you, or the milkman, or the guy who owns the gas station where you take your car to get it filled up. We're talking about the divine.

What do I mean by "divine"? I don't care if you don't even believe in God. If you're an atheist, fine. Because all you don't believe in are the three letters: "G–o–d." But you know there is something big going on—I mean, really big, like the earth swirling around at a huge speed and not even being suspended from a fishing line!

And then there are the moon and the sun and the billions and billions and trillions of stars. That's what I mean when I say that something big is going on. That's what I call "the divine." Because this I know to be true. This I don't have to believe.

There are a lot of beliefs. But I know that what is keeping this universe alive is also in me; it is also keeping me alive. The divine. My divine. Your divine. Our divine. Everywhere making things happen; turning, burning, changing, creating, destroying.

There are a lot of beliefs. But I know that what is keeping this universe alive is also in me, keeping me alive.

From mist—just mist—to floods. All those water droplets, when they rose up, were just a mist. A fog. A vapor. Next thing you know: lightning, thunder, tornadoes, flood! That's my divine. Amazing. From nothing to everything. And that divine, as long as I am alive, is in me. And you have the divine within you as I have the divine within me. And this is the only thing we share.

My skin, as long as it's on me, is mine. And one day it will become dust. Maybe turn into an eggplant, a tomato, or a potato. Everything on this earth is recycled. Very little new material comes in. It's all the same stuff. One day it's taken, put back as

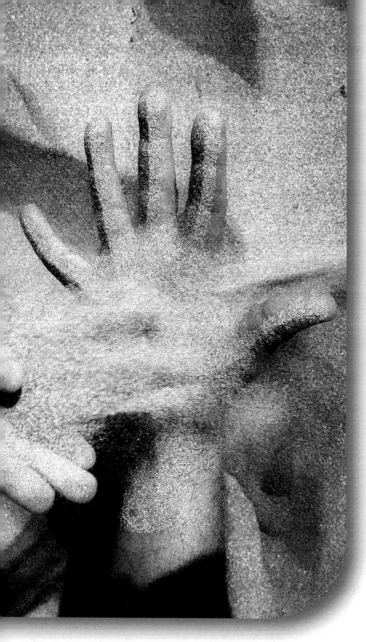

and schedule? Your text messages? People calling you? What does that do for a lot of people? Makes them actually feel good! And if for one day, two days, three days, nobody's calling you, you feel bad.

One day my skin becomes dust.

New things are made out of it.

We don't see it, but that's what's happening.

I know some people think, "What's the big thing about existence? Give me some tools!" I talk about being in love, and there are no tools to fall in love. It's not the perfume, it's not the rituals, it's not the rites, it's not the books, it's not the poems.

Falling in love is something so incredibly different, and there are no tools for it. The first thing you have to be in love with is your life. But it is so alluring to open up one of those slick, fancy magazines and see one of those girls in there. And you say, "How come I don't look like her?"

And you see the picture of the guy resting his hand on the Bentley. It's probably somebody else's. But you say, "That's what I want to be." People look at these "heroes" and say, "Man, he

dust. New things are made out of it. We don't see it, but that's what's happening.

LOVE—NOT TOOLS
Do you understand the significance of being alive, or are you too fascinated by your everyday agenda

110

started from nowhere and nothing, and look what he has accomplished. I want to be just like him." Really? You mean that you haven't learned that being yourself is the most beautiful, the most attractive, the most youthful? After all, you are judged by the company you keep. And if you keep the company of the divine, a little bit of that divinity, believe me, rubs off on you. And you understand, not about a thousand years, but about today. You understand about *now*.

YOUR REALITY

Your reality is right now. And this reality is not about your dreams. It is about what already has been given to you. That's the reality. And where does it begin? Where does peace begin? On top of some mountain? After having read ten thousand books? No.

You open up one of those slick, fancy magazines. And you say, "How come I don't look like her?"

I am talking about reality. Not a fiction, not an ideal, not somebody's idea, but you feeling what the reality is. And the day that begins for you, that is the day you will experience peace. And not temporary peace. Permanent peace. Real peace. And when you experience the real peace, your heart will dance with joy.

You think everything will go silent? "Isn't peace *peaceful*?" No, it really isn't! Peace is nothing like you may have imagined. When you experience peace it is exciting. Every fiber in your body wants to sing with gratitude. Not gratitude for a book, idea, thought, or a person, but gratitude to the divine. That's why I call the divine "divine." Because it is so divine!

And that is the only way I know that there could ever be peace on this earth, because the peace has to begin from the heart, from you. That's why I need to talk about you instead of peace. Peace will naturally happen when all is well with us. The doubt, the fear, the anger; yes, all that's there. But so is joy. So is understanding. So is truth. So is clarity. Isn't it? Then why is it that, year after year, we choose the fear, the doubt, and the anger, instead of the sweet reality that is already inside us?

FEEL IT

That's what I have to say. Feel it. Don't just talk about it. Feel it, because you can. This is your time to feel it, because you're alive, and you just happen to be living in a feeling machine. Of all the things that this "human machine" can do, it can *feel*. Really, really feel. You're in the feeling machine. Get with the feeling. Feel the divine. Let your heart be filled with gratitude. Nothing else is good enough.

What I talk about you know you have experienced in your life. Maybe it was only for a fraction of a second. I want you to experience that which you only experienced for a fraction of a second for the rest of your life. And let the rest of the days of your life be in rejoicing, in understanding, in being fulfilled.

Your reality is right now. And this reality is not about your dreams.

FACT OR FICTION?

WE HAVE BELIEVED IN FICTION FOR SO LONG THAT NOW IT IS ALMOST IMPOSSIBLE TO SEPARATE FACT FROM FICTION.

A fact is a fact; it is what it is. A fiction is somebody's imagination, somebody's idea. You can have as many fictions as you want. You can read books that are fiction. You can watch movies that are fiction, and it's okay. Maybe it's entertaining for a while. But it has no bearing on reality.

There is a clear line that divides fact and fiction. A fact is something real, something that is. It doesn't have to dress itself up. It doesn't have to be bad. It doesn't have to be good. It is what it is. And to me it's very clear that in our lives there is one fact that, if understood and accepted, can bring unimaginable joy, happiness, peace, tranquility, serenity.

So if this is true, why am I concerned about the fiction? The problem is that we have believed in fiction for so long that now it is almost impossible to separate fact from fiction.

I know for a fact I have two eyes. If somebody came to me, really inebriated, really drunk, and said, "You have four eyes!" I don't have to be concerned. I see that he's inebriated, and I am so comfortable in the fact that I have just two eyes that I don't even have to argue with him. I can just say, "It's okay. Go have another drink," or, "Go home. Go to sleep."

TWO DISCOVERIES

In the late 1400s a poet named Kabir was living in India and writing beautiful poems. His poems were not always politically correct, and were challenging for a lot of people, but for others they were very inspiring.

At about the same time, in Spain, Christopher Columbus was setting sail intending to reach East Asia. He landed in the Bahamas and the New World was discovered!

So imagine, by the 1500s there is this poet in India and, about the same time, Christopher Columbus discovers the New World. Meanwhile wars are going on, everybody is looking for peace, everybody is looking for betterment. People want to improve themselves. There is new technology on the horizon that might provide an answer, a freedom. Different expeditions are being launched around the world to discover more.

Up to this point, the depth of people's knowledge was that the earth was flat and that, if you kept going, you would fall off. They didn't *know*, they believed. Today we *know* the earth is round.

So during this multi-stage, multi-story drama, the poet Kabir talks about another kind of discovery, and he says that without self-knowledge you are lost.

Two thousand years before this, Socrates had said, "Know thyself." Socrates and Kabir never met. So why are they on the same page? Why are they both saying, "Know yourself"?

Fact or fiction?

The fact is that every human being, including me, including you, wants to be content. Words don't matter. Call it "happiness." Call it "joy." Call it "peace," call it "truth." If you're extra spiritual, call it something else. If you're nonspiritual, call it something else. If you're modern, call it something else. If you're deeply religious, call it something else. It's just semantics.

If four people viewing an elephant seem to be describing the elephant differently, the question to ask is, "Where were you standing?" Because, believe me, an elephant looks very different from the front than the back. And so people say, "I think this way." "I think that way." Have you not heard people say that? "I think!" That's their mantra! "Think-think-think-think!"

But then there is knowing, and Kabir says that without knowing who you are, you are lost.

Kabir says that without knowledge of the self we are like the musk deer that roams around the forest, searching for the musk, searching for the source of that wonderful smell, and cannot find it even though the scent comes from its own navel. And because the musk deer cannot find that source, it searches again and again and again and again and again. And not finding it, the deer is sad.

The fact is that every human being, including me, including you, wants to be content.

How does Kabir describe the situation of the world? The analogy he gives is that the world is like a flower. And all the bees are coming and going, coming and going, coming and going to the flower. Coming in, touching down, going out, buzzing around the flower. He says that in the same way, the mind is buzzing! And who did this apply to? Who does this apply to?

He says, "Everybody!" Oh yes, even the ones that sit very still: *"Bzzzz-bzzzz!"* The thoughts are going on and on and on: "What time is it?" "What is it?" "Why is this this way?" "Why is that that way?" "Why?" "Why me, God?" "Why couldn't I be the king?" "Why do I have to sit here?" *"Bzzzz!"*

You look around the world and when things don't make sense, what is the answer you get? "God works in mysterious ways."

That's it? That's your answer?

If you ordered toast and they brought you burnt toast, you might ask, "Why did you bring burnt toast?" Would you expect the waiter's answer to be "We work in mysterious ways"? That's it? I mean, that's *it*? The police officer pulls you over: "Why were you speeding?" "I work in mysterious ways." I mean, that's it? Fiction!

What is reality? It is so obvious. And it is so beautiful. It is! From sunrise to sunset, from the clouds to the birds, to the ocean, to the lakes, to the summits, to the snow, from the deserts to the green pastures, it is so beautiful. And this is why I'm saying all this.

WHAT IS YOURS?

We have at least two gentlemen who have said you should know yourself. Why? Why should I know myself? You know your name, right? So you know yourself? No. They didn't say, "You should know your name." Should you know your face? No. Your height? No. Your weight? No. Your resumé?

I have to read a lot of resumés. And they always make me laugh. Because you cannot have that much lying on a piece of paper anywhere else. There are actually courses you can take to learn how to fill out your resumé so that it looks like you worked for God, directly, and you have infinite powers that you cannot even talk about.

What is it, this "Know thyself"? Fact: My body is dirt. There's no question about that. It's made of dirt. Fact: It's recycled. The composition is new, but it's recycled dirt. That's what happens on this earth. Now everybody's starting to go "green." They say, "We should recycle!" But this creation has been recycling for a really long time. It takes the dirt, squeezes it a little bit and it becomes a rock. Then what happens to the rock? It becomes dirt again. And the water comes along, takes it from here to there. The wind comes along, takes it from there to there. And these minerals and these components make up your body.

And water! I'm 70% water. You are 70% water. New composition—the way you look, the way you talk, the way you think—but recycled. So this body that you call your own is not your own. Is that fact or fiction? You don't have to answer me. Just think about it.

You live in a house or an apartment. Do you call it your own? Unless you built that apartment or that house, somebody else lived there before you. And those people called it their own. And maybe one day you will move on, and somebody else will move in, and they will call it their own. Fact or fiction? Whose is it? For a period of time you can call it your own. But then there will be many others who will own, own, own, own.

People work so hard: "I hope I will be remembered!" Will you? Do you remember all those people who aspired to be remembered? You don't even know who they were!

Will this earth be gone one day? Fact or fiction? Fact: it'll be gone. Will the sun be gone? Fact or fiction? It'll be gone. Should you know yourself? Fact or fiction? Fact! Because your thirst, your desire to be content, will only be quenched when you realize what the truth is. Not before that.

What is the truth? It is my great pleasure, my privilege, to introduce you to the truth. Are you ready? It is simple and it is profound. The truth is you are alive!

YOU ARE RELATED

Do you have any idea what it means to be alive? It's the miracle of miracles, unbelievable, unimaginable, that the breath, this gift, comes into you courtesy of the divine: that power that sustains this universe; that makes it possible for the dirt to be compressed to form heavenly bodies, then forces their vectors for collision so they become dust again, to be formed again; the same power that makes it possible for stars to be where they are and to glow, every twinkle in the heavens, every little touch of wind on the earth, every drop of water, every grain of sand.

What is the truth? It is simple and it is profound.

The truth is you are alive!

If you were related to Columbus, would you feel proud? Do you know who you're related to? You're related—in the truest sense of the word, you're related to the divine. Fact or fiction? Fact. The same power that creates galaxies, created this earth, created your mother, created your father, created you. Fact or fiction?

And within you is this divine. And you should not take my word for it. This is why I love going around the world talking to people, because I get to tell them, "The divine is within you—and don't believe *me!* It's a fact."

You are alive: Fact. You have been given a gift: Fact. You are related to the divine: Fact. You are the most blessed: Fact? Don't believe me. It's not fiction. It's fact. The key is, you should find out for yourself.

Some people say, "Well, what is the proof?" Where do your proofs come from? Books. People say, "It is written!" Your proof should not come from a book, but from you knowing for yourself.

Last night I made a pasta dish. And I could have just tasted it and said to the person helping me, "Mmm! It's really good! It tastes like this and it tastes like this." But I wanted them to taste it too. And when they did? "Wow! That's good!" That's the kind of proof I'm talking about.

You can know the reality that is shining within you, because it's fact, not fiction. You can understand that you are the source of your comfort: Fact, not fiction. Within you is your heart. And the heart is the place where the reality dwells. And reality and truth, and that magnificence, that divinity, are beautiful. Truth is not ugly. The truth is beautiful. And what is it? What is your truth? What is my truth? I am alive. You are alive. You find that ugly? I don't.

We think riches make a person happy and poverty makes a person sad. When you were born, what was your wealth? As soon as you took the first breath, there was only one thing you had, and that was your existence. You existed! Your existence was the only thing you owned. And when your last minute comes, that's all you're going to want: Existence!

What do you have right now that's truly yours? Your existence. Do you know how to enjoy it? Do you know how to understand it? Fact or fiction?

Everything I have said, you know. You have always known. But you have looked at other things and briefly been entertained. We were all once addicted to knowing. Believing meant nothing to you, nothing! You would not buy into believing even for one second.

There were times you wanted your mother's attention when you were very, very young. And if your mother said to you, "Just make believe I'm there." *"No!"* "Make believe you're full." *"No!"* "Make believe you're fine." *"No!"*

What do you have that's truly yours?

Your existence.

Do you know how to enjoy it?

Do you know how to understand it?

And then, slowly, as we grew older, and older, and older, we became believers. And not only did we become believers, we were very proud to be believers: "Oh, you have made a believer out of me!"

FACTS MATTER

I don't want to make a believer out of you. I want you to be a knower, someone who knows the value of breath, the value of existence. Because then, and only then, will you know what gratitude is.

And when your heart is filled with gratitude you can give thanks. "Thank you for this life!" And you don't care who you're addressing this to. Should you begin thanking now, or should you wait till the very end? Begin every single day.

That's all I have to say. I just want to sort fact from fiction. There's too much fiction around. Fact is what's going to matter in your life.

You can know the reality that is shining within you.
Because it's fact, not fiction.

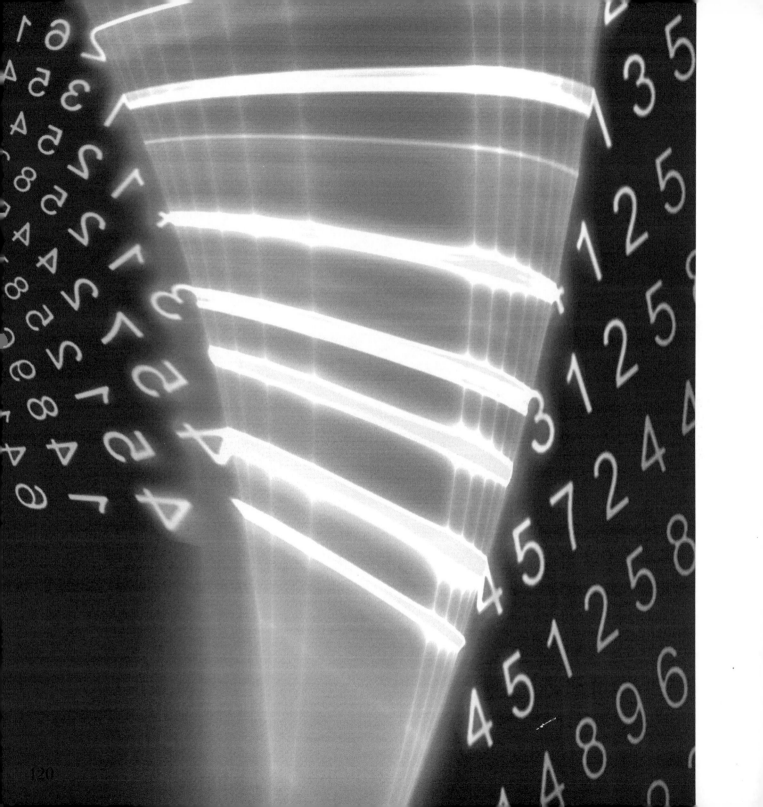

PART FOUR

THE STRATEGY

You should have peace.
You should have joy.
You should have contentment.

And if you don't,
change the strategy.

**Next time you see "You are here,"
think about it.
Because you ARE here.**

HOW MANY THINGS DO YOU KNOW, AND HOW MANY THINGS DO YOU BELIEVE? SCARY QUESTION.

SYMPTOMS OF CONFUSION

We look at the world around us—wars going on, debates, police, military. Political crisis. All these things are happening because there is a disease. And if you have a disease it's going to produce a symptom. You may not like the symptom, but the best way to get rid of the symptom is to diagnose the disease, and then get rid of it.

You look at all the problems that exist in the world. For example, children being abandoned. How could that happen? People going hungry when there's really no shortage of food. How could that happen? People fighting each other over the stupidest, stupidest things. And you start to see a picture emerge, and you realize that these are merely the symptoms.

I see this picture of restlessness, of non-understanding. It's like when a dog forgets to be a dog. There's a TV show where they show you dogs misbehaving. The dog thinks he is the owner and that the owner is the dog. He wants the owner to be submissive. He bites the owner. The owner is afraid of his own dog. The dog rips up every pillow, rips up the sofa, does things that a dog is not supposed to do, but he does them because somehow the dog has forgotten its place.

So I ask a simple question. Could it be, looking at the symptoms of the world, that we human beings have forgotten who we are? And then what goes out the window? The human being's humanity. The value of life. Evolving no longer has a point or purpose.

If a train is running nicely on the tracks and you add another engine, it'll go faster, because now there are two engines pushing it. But if the train is derailed and you attach another engine to it, you're only going to make the situation worse.

We humans have forgotten who we are.

And then what goes out the window?

The humanity. The value of life.

Now you may be thinking, "Are you saying that there should be no military? There should be no this? There should be no that?" No, I'm not saying that. You may be saying that. I'm saying, "Could we evolve to a point where we could talk first?"

One of the nations has come up with a new one: "Preemptive strike." If that's the way the world really worked, nothing would function. The policeman would hand you a ticket every time he saw you. "You might be speeding!" Or, as soon as you park your car, your windshield is full of tickets: "Preemptive strike!"

BREATH IS THE MIRACLE

So who are we? On one hand, we are nothing special. Do we listen? Not really. Are we good at swimming? No. Walking? Not really that good. Mountain climbing? Nothing like the goats. Flying? We're bad at it. So what are we really good at? And this is what makes us who we are: we have the ability to experience the beauty, the joy that resides in the heart of every single human being. That's what we're good at.

Maybe you're thinking, "What about the sheep, and the goat, and all the other animals?" I don't know about them. I've never had a deep conversation with a goat, or a sheep, or a camel. But with you I can. You are like I am: a human being.

And how does it begin for us? It begins very simply. The symphony of life truly begins with the first breath. If you are born in a hospital, if you take that breath, you get to come home. If you don't take that breath, you don't get to come home.

That first breath is the simplest of all actions—and yet, the most profound. Profound, because that's where it begins. Profound, because it keeps happening throughout your existence. Profound, because when it stops, you no longer exist.

I know some people are thinking, "Yeah, but I can hold my breath." It's really amazing what happens if you do manage to keep holding your breath—you will pass out! And then you start breathing normally.

Because of something that is happening, *you* are happening. When it is not happening, you are not happening. All this time we breathe—but we pay no attention. We breathe—we pay no attention. It doesn't matter to us. We've got our agenda. We've got this to do. We've got that to do. That's where our focus is.

And then way too soon comes the day when the breath is no more. And that's what the doctor checks. Oh, he's got all the electronic equipment and everything else. But the doctor knows those machines sometimes get undone and declare you dead when you are not. And then the alarms go off. The nurse comes around saying, "Oh! Okay, okay. This just fell off." But the last check is always: "Are you still breathing?" If you are, "Good."

The breath is the miracle of all miracles. What is a miracle to people? A rock bleeding. A frog talking. "Wow!" Unusual things happening are miraculous. What's normal isn't.

Somebody said to me, "Oh, I am sorry it is raining"—because it was raining outside. I said, "Did you do this?" And he said, "No, no, no." I said, "I don't know why people think it is so bad when it rains. It is the purest gift from the heavens, the purest. Don't forget you're seventy percent water. How can you be sorry for some more water?"

And it's pure. As pure as it gets. Pristine. The giver of life to everything. But we forget. Why? Because it gets in the way of our socialization: "Now the hairdo that took me seven hours to put together is going to go flat because of the rain." And when you were a little kid, did the rain stop you? No. You would go out and *run* in the rain.

THE CHOICE

Sometimes I wonder if a person is wiser when they are young or if it is the other way. When you were little you lived for the day. That's all that mattered. I remember lying in bed waiting for the morning to come. And when was the morning going to come? When there was light. And all it took was the smallest inkling through a window, a little crack somewhere to let the light in—and I was up.

Every human being has so much to be unthankful for, and every human being has so much to be thankful for. What do we choose? You have to make a choice every single day. And what do you choose? Do you choose gratitude? If you want gratitude in your life, there is only one way you're going to receive gratitude. And that is if you have clarity. If you are wallowing in doubt, that is a disease. And the symptom is confusion. Is there a cure for this disease? Yes! Thankfully, yes, there is a known cure for this disease, and it is called clarity.

What are the symptoms of confusion? Confusion will always lead to pain. And human beings cannot tolerate pain. Oh yes, in India you see all these guys driving a nail through their tongue. But if they break their leg? Straight to the medical emergency: "Oh, please look at me, my leg really hurts so bad." People walking on fire? It's a trick. It's not like they have conquered any pain. That would be wrong. Pain was created to get your attention, because otherwise you would pay no attention to fixing the problem.

You have to choose every single day how you want that day to be. And it takes a lot. Sometimes it's beyond human capacity to keep it together.

But it is better to remember and try again and again and again, than never to try at all, and not know in your life what you are capable of feeling.

What are the symptoms of confusion?

Confusion always leads to pain. And we cannot tolerate pain.

As a human being, I have the privilege of feeling peace. And what is peace? Peace is when all that is within—the heart, the understanding, and the clarity—is healthy. Healthy! Not just disease-free but healthy. There's a big difference.

Healthy is when you are in good shape. Of course, people run, and they diet. And dieting is hard, because there are all these wonderful things— ice cream, cakes, donuts, fried food, butter. And you know that if you eat them, it's not so good. Then you will have to exercise. So you diet.

JUNK FOOD FOR THE SELF

Do you also diet for your mind? For your self? How fat is your confusion? In the realm of the inner self, how out of shape are you? What have you been feeding it? Junk food!

How many things do you know, and how many things do you believe? Scary question. And how many things do you think you know, because you have believed them for so long? Even scarier.

126

I like books, but I cannot understand this fascination people have with them. If you cannot convince people of the garbage that you *want* to convince them of—all you have to do is print it in a book. Because if something is printed in black on this white thing called paper, it automatically becomes the truth.

It's a similar phenomenon—when the phone rings, people drop everything to pick up the phone. It becomes a matter of life and death. I've seen people really go through it. They're talking to me. If somebody else comes into the room, they will not be disturbed by it. It's like, "No. Just wait a minute. I'm talking to him." Then their phone rings—and I'm nothing! "Hello?"

You could be with the people who are most precious to you—your mother, your father, your wife, your children. You're having a big family reunion. The phone rings. You'll drop all of them—to pick it up. Why? Because it is a habit.

In the realm of the inner self, how out of shape are you? How fat is your confusion?

Is it a good habit? Is it a bad habit? Doesn't matter. It's not up to me to decide that. A habit happens by repetition. Sometimes from an unconscious thought. Do it enough times and it becomes a habit.

How many things do you do without thinking about them? Somebody says to you, "How are you?" You say, "Fine." Are you? You may not be—but it's a stranger: "I'm fine. How are you?" Do you really want to know? No. Absolutely not. You're never going to meet this person again in your whole life. But manners, habit—"How are you?" "Oh, yeah, I'm good. And how are you?"

So what else do you believe in? You've been fed many lines: "Study, study, study. Work, work, work. Retire, retire, retire. Die, die, die." I see people retire, and they go crazy. They can't retire. They have to do something.

SINGING DUST

What I say is, "Live, live, live. Thrive. Be alive till you are no more. Understand the gift that every day is for you. It's for *you!*" The saga of the sun rising in the east and setting in the west has played out on this planet earth for millions and millions of years. Countless winters have come; countless summers have come. So what's special about this summer? You are here!

You look at yourself. You think you're brand-new. You are not. Very little new matter comes to the earth anymore. It's all recycled. All of it. All that stuff you clean up at home, what do you think that is? Most of it is skin; dead, dry skin. That's what dust is. "Dust to dust," they say. The miracle is when the dust is breathing. When it's thinking. When it's alive. When it loves. You are dust that can love. That can feel. That can sing. Even though you don't know how to sing, you can sing. There's another *singing*. It's the singing inside, called happiness.

"Dust to dust," they say. The miracle is when the dust is breathing. When it's alive.

When it's thinking. When it loves.

You are dust that can love. That can feel. That can sing.

You can feel joy. "You" is the key word here. *You* can feel joy. And joy is so special that, if you're not feeling it, something is wrong. It's a disease.

Is there a cure? Yes, there is. When you hear that Socrates said, "Know thyself," does that sound like an answer to you, or a question? That's an answer to your questions. And you might say, "You don't even know me or know what my questions are." I don't have to. I know exactly how big your problems are: the size of your head. That is how big your problems are.

When there is contentment dancing inside, all is well. And when that contentment is not dancing, all is not well. It is in that realm of wellness that peace exists, accessible to every human being on the face of this earth. The key lies in knowing yourself. Only when you know yourself can you truly answer the question "How are you?" Because then, and only then, you would know how you are supposed to be.

This is the time of the divinity dancing inside. And as long as that divinity is dancing inside, shouldn't all be well? And shouldn't you feel that wellness, that peace, that gratitude, that clarity, that understanding, that joy in your life?

THE STORMS

Here is the other big issue. Will storms come in your life? Yes, absolutely. Will confusion knock at your door? Absolutely. And will you be in traumatic situations—some of them not even in your control? Absolutely. But remember this. Even when the biggest storm is going on, when the biggest chaos is afoot, when the night is as dark as it gets, there is still a lamp lit inside you. I will not underestimate how bad the situations can be, but as long as the breath is coming in and out of you, you have the companionship of the divine.

When you feel weak—and that's what the storms do, they weaken you—know that the greatest strength lies within you. There's nothing stronger than the divine. The same divine creates, destroys, sustains the universe, known and unknown, explored, and not yet explored. It keeps the earth suspended without strings, without pillars. In its creation, all is well. The sun is there, the moon, the earth, quadrillions and quadrillions of stars in the galaxies are there. And all things are rotating, and coming together, and going this way, and going that way, and getting blasted to dust, and then composed again into a planet, and all is well.

It needs to be like that in your universe: everything moving, but at the same time, all is well. Coming, going, yes. There is chaos out there, and there is order out there. And you are here.

Sometimes I go to shopping malls. They have a map that says, "You are here." I like that. Next time you are in a shopping mall and you see "You are here", think about it. Because you *are* here. And you can explore all the joys that lie within your heart. And peace will be yours. You have more peace in you than you can possibly imagine.

People take notes: "What can I do to become a better person?" Stop wasting paper. Whatever you can write down is not what's going to help you become a better person, believe me. What makes you a good person is not writable—it's *feel-able*. Clarity makes you a better person. Understanding makes you a better person. Discovering your kindness makes you a better person.

You have been given everything you need. You have the tools. Discover! Dig! Dig! Dig! And you will find the treasure. Because there is a treasure in you.

As long as you are alive, that's the opportunity—whether you take it or not is up to you.

You have been given everything you need. You have the tools. Discover! Dig! And you will find the treasure. Because there is a treasure in you.

STRANGERS IN A STRANGE WORLD

WE DISREGARD THE REALITY THAT IS STARING US IN THE FACE. COULD IT BE ANY STRANGER THAN THAT?

Here we are, strangers in a very strange world, trying to find something that's familiar and not strange. But we forget that we are strangers—all of us. We try to identify with each other by our friendships, by "I know your face; I know your name; I know who you are." But that's not true, because one day, you might discover something about another person that you never thought possible.

And the world is also very strange. In this world, if people want to do something that even God would not forgive, then they do it in the name of religion. Unimaginable things have happened in the name of God.

Everybody tells you there is only one God, and then there are all these people who tell you, "If you want to believe in God, this is how you do it." Now why would you need any training to believe in God anyway? Because it's just about *believing*. It's not about *knowing* God.

WHO IS YOUR FRIEND?
In this strange world, you are not the owner.

You're only renting. One day your agreement for the rent will expire, and that will be it. You have to move on. Where will you go? No one knows. Is there speculation? Of course. But it's all hearsay. Hearsay is not allowed in a court of law. It's not admissible. But how many people in this world do you think believe hearsay? Just about everybody. "I heard someone said this." "I heard someone said that."

We're searching for peace, and in trying to find some sanctuary, some meaning, some answer—something logical about this incredibly illogical world—we embrace that which is speculation. It sparks our fantasy. We ignore that which is true. And we disregard the reality that is staring us in the face. Could it be any stranger than that?

What is the reality? Who is your friend in this strange world? You try to strike up a friendship: "Let me find a friend." Aren't friends important? Well, who is your friend? The coming and going of the breath is your friend. It heralds life. It heralds the existence of the divine in this human vessel. This is not hearsay. This is a reality that you will know for yourself when you remove all the hearsay. The fundamental difference between knowing and believing is not much. It's as thin as a single hair, as fine as a blade, but it makes a complete difference.

All your life people have told you things, and you have believed them because you are trapped by ideas—chains that hold you back, and each link in the chain is the very hearsay and beliefs you have accumulated.

HAPPY THEN SAD

I know this sounds intense—it *is*. But everything that I speak about basically boils down to this: You have a choice. In my experience, one of two things happens that seems to be the ultimate result of all the things that occur in your life. And this is not hearsay. I am sure you have experienced the same, since you're not different from me. Whatever you do ultimately makes you either happy or unhappy. If it makes you happy, you like it. If it makes you unhappy, you don't like it.

Let's say you pack your backpack and take a trip to the mountains to go climbing, to enjoy nature, and soon you're enjoying, and enjoying, and enjoying. Then all of a sudden you're lost. And now you are not enjoying. Well, wait a minute. Two days ago you were enjoying this exact activity. You were in the middle of the mountains with nobody around, and you said, "Wow! Nature!" Two days later, snow is falling; wind is blowing a hundred miles an hour. It's still nature, but now you are not enjoying it.

So two days: enjoy, enjoy, enjoy. Next two days: "I hate this. I'm so stupid. Why did I come out here? This is terrible." If you are lucky, somebody rescues you. If you are not lucky, you die. After you're dead, you don't get to enjoy, and you don't get to complain. You don't get to laugh, and you don't get to cry. Maybe the helicopter comes, and everybody on the ground is yelling, "Help!" but the rescuers can't hear it. The helicopter is so noisy that they wear headphones to kill the sound from the outside. And you are down there screaming, "Help!" Fortunately, if they can see you, maybe they can rescue you—maybe. And when you get rescued, you become very happy: "Oh, thank you. Thank you."

Happy and then sad. And then happy. And then sad. Why do you forget that that's what has been going on all your life? My advice is—and this is just my advice—when you get happy, don't forget the sad times. And when you get sad, don't forget the happy times. Remember just enough to remind you—no more than that. Don't start thinking, "Oh, my God. I'm happy, so the sad times are just around the corner." No. Just remember enough to have sanity. That's what sanity is—to enjoy and do nothing to end up in the sad times.

I have talked to so many people who were shocked by life. Why is life a shock to people? Have you ever wondered? That's what happens when you believe and don't know. When you know, you understand one thing: There are two options at the end of the day—sadness or happiness. Pick one. It's a simple formula: Do as much as possible to have happiness in your life. And if you are truly a follower of happiness, if happiness is your dream, if happiness is your desire, then knowledge of the self can bring you the truest happiness there is.

ARE YOU HOLY?

Who do you think made this earth? Was it you? Your grandfather? Your great-grandfather? Your neighbors? It was the power that some call God and some don't. It doesn't matter to that power what you call it. Why should it care? You didn't create the power. The power created you. So I have some questions.

One day you have to move on. Where will you go? No one knows.

If that divine power created this earth, wouldn't this earth be divine? And wouldn't this earth be heaven? How could it not be? And what do we do? We spit on it. Why? Because we believe that heaven is "up there," not down here.

Who is holy? Are you holy? You may say, "No, no, no. Somebody who has dedicated their life to God is holy, not me." Isn't God in you? So if

God is in you, and even if you didn't want to be holy, wouldn't you be holy? How could you not be holy?

The divine wants to dance with you. But first you have to hear the music—not the music *you* make and not the music the world makes. When I say "strangers in a strange world," this should sound very strange. But it doesn't. It actually makes sense. Because until you have heard the rhythm that plays inside you, you have not heard the music of the divine. Your heart yearns to dance. Your heart yearns to know. Your heart yearns to feel. And until it can, it all seems very strange.

KNOWLEDGE OF THE SELF

Sometimes you feel strong and powerful. And sometimes you feel weak and insignificant. Which one is really you—the powerful or the insignificant? It doesn't take much to make you feel powerful, and it doesn't take much to make you feel insignificant. Which one are you? Until you know, it's all going to feel very strange, because, in reality, that powerful one is not you. And that insignificant one is not you either. You are something else.

You are a vessel that yearns to sing within with the rhythm of the divine, with the joy that comes from feeling peace in your existence. Filled—not empty. Distant from questions. You find your home when you are lost in fulfillment. You begin to live when you are drowning in peace.

Then, amazingly enough, you understand what it means to be alive. You will never be able to express what it feels like to be fulfilled. There are no words. There is no way you could ever say what it feels like—if you are fulfilled. You get lost in the feeling. And in this being lost, you find yourself.

If you are not fulfilled, but just believe you are fulfilled, you will go on and on: "It's like this; it's like that," and it will all be garbage. This is why it has been said, "Those who know it can't say it. And those who don't know it say it all."

Your heart yearns to dance. Your heart yearns to know. Your heart yearns to feel.

And until it can, it all seems very strange.

When you love someone, you say, "I love you." What does that mean? People use the word "love" about all sorts of things, like food, cars, even nail polish. When something really means something to you, when something is really dear to you, when something is real to you, it cannot be expressed. When something is so beautifully consuming that it commands your heart, you get lost in the feeling. But in this "lost," you find yourself. In the world, you also get lost, but in *that* lost, you lose yourself.

Happiness or sorrow? Pick one. I hope it will be happiness; I hope it will be joy. And once you've picked it, I hope you will do everything possible to get it. It's a good formula. It works. It requires consciousness. And to be conscious, you need to have peace. If you don't have peace, it's very hard to be conscious of anything.

You don't know who you are. That's why you are a stranger. It's not because other people don't know who you are. That doesn't matter. It's because *you* don't know who you are. Some people want to introduce you to everyone. I want to introduce you to you. In your opinion, it may be easier to know others than to know yourself. In my opinion, it is hard to know others and easy to know your self. Even those you think you know will prove that they are strangers. Sooner or later, they will do something you won't believe. "I thought I knew that person!" You *thought* you knew. That doesn't count.

So we've got to stop this strange thing of being a stranger. When you are introduced to you, you can find the true friend within, and you will not be a stranger anymore. When you find your true world, you won't be a stranger in this world anymore.

You don't know who you are. That's why you are a stranger.

You find your home when you are lost in fulfillment. You begin to live when you are drowning in peace.

WIN THE WAR

IN YOUR LIFE YOU HAVE MANY BATTLES, BUT ONLY ONE WAR. WHAT IS THIS WAR? AND HOW DO YOU WIN IT?

You have your battles and you have the war. Now you might be thinking, "Shouldn't it be 'wars' plural?" No. You will have many battles. But you have only one war. And as vulnerable as we are as human beings, we fight the battles but forget about the war. We get so concerned about the battles: "Got to win this, got to win that." And if we lose a battle, we say, "Oh, my God, that's it. I've lost everything." No, you haven't!

If you lose a battle, no problem. Try again! As long as you haven't lost the war, you can fight as many battles as you want. Retreat; try again tomorrow. Get a bigger sword—whatever you can do. But once you have lost the war, that's another story.

So what are these battles? And what is the war? All the things that happen in our lives—the good and the bad—are the battles. And how do I know that people are extremely concerned about their battles? Recently the plug was pulled out of the bathtub, and all the water started to drain out really fast. I'm talking about the financial crisis! Actually, the plug had been leaking for quite a few years. But somebody kept putting another bucket of water in there, so it never looked like anything was happening. But then all of a sudden somebody really pulled the plug, and the water went down very fast. Some people jumped out of office buildings because they thought they were finished. They lost the battle, and with that battle, they also lost the war. They could have easily lost that battle and then won again. And lost another one, and won again. But once you lose the war, that's it.

WHAT IS THE WAR?

So now the question is, what is the war? And how do you win it?

Because of our arrogance we fail to see the reality that in each human being lies the source of peace. In each human being lies divinity, beauty, the source of fulfillment. In each one of us. But you have to be humble enough to see that. If you look through the glasses of arrogance, that's not what you will see. What you will see is, "Me? I'm here. I have to do this; I have to do this; I have to do this. And after that, if I do this, and this, and this, I'll go to heaven."

In our arrogance we claim heaven. Where is that heaven? Away from us. Who will get there? Those who make good grades. But drop the glasses of arrogance, and you will see that the heaven you are looking for is right here—not anywhere else.

Somebody might say, "Ah. You mean to tell me that good-for-nothing person is in heaven?!" Yes. But if that person doesn't know that, are they? I'm talking about knowing, not believing.

Because of our arrogance we fail to see that in each human being lies the source of peace.

In each human being lies divinity, beauty, the source of fulfillment.

Do you *know* that in you the most beautiful is taking place? It's the coming and going of the breath. In you is the source—the immortal source of peace. You are blessed in every way possible.

And knowing that and being able to feel it every day is winning the war.

You have battles in relationships. People get upset with you; you get upset with them, and you make up. But do you know that there is a battle you lose every day because you do not recognize the beauty that is inside of you? And ultimately, if you keep losing that battle and end up losing the war, you truly will have come into this world empty-handed and you will leave empty-handed. Having everything and having saved nothing. Having everything and not having savored anything. Having a house next to the purest water and dying of thirst. That, truly, is a tragedy.

NOT LOOKING?

When I say these things about peace being inside of you, joy being inside of you—that, indeed, what you are looking for is inside of you—a lot of people say, "I'm not looking for anything." Let me ask you a question: When you wake up in the morning, what do you do? Do you just lie there in bed till you can confirm it's 11:00 PM again and then go back to sleep, or do you get up?

Maybe the first thing you go for is a cup of coffee or tea. Maybe you get ready to jog. Maybe you take a shower. Maybe you get ready to go to work. Do you realize that within you have a mechanism that says, "Arise"? And this is so fundamental that it existed before people had jobs. This "Arise" isn't so that you can get to work. This "Arise" is saying, "Enough sleep already! Get up! Get on with being alive!" If you have any doubt about it, look at a baby.

Not long ago, our family had the great fortune to welcome another member. And so I am a grandfather. Nothing actually happened to me. I just stood there taking pictures. It wasn't that I became a grandfather. No, what happened was our baby had a baby.

And I have been observing this baby. Sometimes he's sleeping. Sometimes he is smiling, cooing, trying to talk. Going at it. Moving his hands, looking around. And sometimes he's crying, "Waah!" He doesn't express exactly what it is he needs. He just goes "Waah," and somehow his mother knows what to do, and he calms down and goes back to sleep.

I was tickling him, and he just started to smile, babbling, "Ga-ga, goo-goo." And I kept doing it, and he kept smiling, and he almost wanted to laugh. And then I thought about it: Laugh, smile, as much as you can. Because right now when you have a need, you merely say, "Waah." But as you get older, this cry gets much more buried. You will have a need, but you are going to express it in infinite ways.

The fact that you have a need isn't going to change. The way you express it is going to change. The way you are entertained is going to change. It isn't going to be your grandfather tickling you on your cheeks, and you saying, "Ga-ga, goo-goo." It might be your girlfriend doing a similar thing, and you saying a similar thing, but it won't be "Ga-ga, goo-goo." It'll be a little bit more than that. Right now, it's "Ga-ga, goo-goo," and then it's going to turn into "I love you."

The fact that you need to like and that you need to express what you like is not going to change. With the frustrations that you will have, the "Waah" is going to become very refined. It's going to go from "Waah" to "What's the matter with you?" But the root of it is going to be the same: that little anger . . .

My grandson turns all red, as if to say, "Uuugh! I need to let you know things aren't right." And that's not going to change. How it is done will go through incredible nuances. This is the story of your life, and this is the story of my life. We think we are getting older? All we do is refine what we have always done.

THE CONNECTION

Do you have a need? Absolutely. And every day you go satisfaction hunting. And there are a lot of very smart people—at least that's what they consider themselves to be—who know that you are looking for something, even when you say you're not. The advertising industry is worth billions and billions and billions of dollars, because they know you are vulnerable and you are looking. You are looking, and you are searching, and if they put a colorful billboard up there, you will look up at it and say, "That's what I need!"

In magazine after magazine, newspaper after newspaper, advertisers count on you being vulnerable, because if you weren't looking, there would be no reason for them to advertise. But they know that in between reading the news, you are looking. All they have to do is grab your attention.

The question is, do you know what you're looking for?

There was a moment when this baby was born. Suddenly, there he was. He didn't know. The nurse took him and dried him off, and then he was put on his mother's stomach. And, as little as he was, he lifted his head, opened his eyes, and looked at his mother. In that moment I knew his loneliness ended. Up till that point there was nothing he could connect with. I don't know if he could see anything except gobs of light, but if you looked in his eyes, you could see that he looked at her. Maybe he could smell; maybe he could hear. There she was and he made a beautiful connection. And from then on in his life, everything is taken care of.

You and I, we have grown up with that need to make the connection, and it is still there. What I am looking for, what you are looking for, is to find the connection within ourselves. Not to a face, but to a feeling that is real, that is true. To the true understanding of what it is to be alive.

Some people say, "Oh, you talk about death." No, all I say about death is that it is inevitable. But I don't get into it, because my message is not about death; it's about life. It's about right now. What did today bring you? What did yesterday bring you? What can tomorrow bring you? Do you have any idea? Tomorrow holds the promise of the fulfillment of a lifetime. Today holds the promise of the fulfillment of a lifetime. Yesterday held the promise of the fulfillment of a lifetime. That's what every day is about.

What I am looking for, what you are looking for, is to find the connection within ourselves.

Not to a face, but to a feeling that is real, that is true.

THE CHOICE

When we get into emergency situations, the first thing that goes is our arrogance. Up until then we say things like, "That is not my name. Please pronounce my name correctly!" Then you find yourself trapped in an elevator, sandwiched between two floors, and what do you scream? "Help *me!*" No name, nothing—no etiquette. Just, "Help me! Can anyone hear me?"

This *me* is your reality. And as long as you remember that, you will do well for yourself. Understand and remember that it is this me who has come into this world and it is this me who one day has to go. It is this me who has the desire to be fulfilled and it is this me who needs to be fulfilled, and it is this me who may lose quite a few battles. But this me needs—*needs*—to win the war.

There are so many who help people win battles. "Let me read your horoscope. When were you born? Let me see what today will be like. That planet is over there, and that planet is over there, so wear yellow today and don't sign any contracts." Yes, there are plenty of people waiting to help you win the battles. And they've got you so absorbed in trying to win the battles, that you have forgotten about the war. And so I come along and I say, "By the way, forget about the battles; let's win the war." And everybody says, "What are you talking about? What war? I thought it was all just battles." No. If you're in a battle, believe me, there is a war.

And the war has to be won. Do you want to win the war? That's the bottom line. You have to choose.

Doing the same thing again and again in your life and expecting a different result is not going to work. When people do that it's a little rocky for them, to say the least. They keep going on in the same grind, hoping that one day everything will change. How? If you want change, you have to make a choice. Do you want peace in your life? You have to make the choice.

BUDDHA

People say, "Is it that easy? No searching? No going to the top of the Himalayas? No surrendering of everything? No burying your head in the snow for eight years? None of that stuff?" Of course, if you want to do that, it's all possible. I'm sure somebody will be happy to accommodate you. It won't be me. I don't like cold weather. And I don't want to bury my head in the snow for eight years. I'm not coming with you.

It's easy just to say, "It is so because it is written." Well, what is *your* choice? My father used to ask, "What was Buddha's grandfather's religion?" Think about it. He couldn't have been a Buddhist. Buddha wasn't around yet.

When Buddha was born, the astrologer said to the king, "He's going to be a great king or a great saint." His father didn't want him to be a saint; he wanted him to be a king. So he cut him off from anything spiritual.

One day, when Buddha sneaks out with his servant, he sees a poor person. He's never seen a poor person in his life, so he asks:

"Who is he?"
"He's poor."

"Poor? What's a 'poor'?"
"Well, he doesn't have enough money."

"Money? What is 'money'?"
"Oh, well, some are fortunate. You are fortunate, Prince. You have a lot of money; you are a prince. He is not; he is a beggar."

"Nobody told me about 'fortunate.' What is that?"

He walks on a little bit farther, and he sees a body lying there.

"Who's he?"
"He's dead."

"Dead? What's a 'dead'?"
"He's not living anymore."

"Living? Am I living?"
"Yes, you are."

"Is 'dead' what's going to happen to me?"
"Yes."

One day changes his whole way of thinking. And he makes a choice. He says, "I want to find something that is above and beyond this fortunate business, and poor business, and rich business, and death business—I don't want any part of all that. There must be something better."

Yes, there is. And it's inside of you. It comes with every breath. This life, this existence, this grace, this blessing. The breath comes in and out of us, and we pay no attention. What if divinity expresses itself in the form of the breath that comes in and out of you? I just said, "what if." That's to be kind. I put the question in your head—not the answer. But I know the answer because I have felt it. What I say comes not from a book, but from my own experience of *knowing*—not contemplating.

141

One day changes his whole way of thinking.

He says, "I want to find something that is above and beyond this fortunate business, and poor business, and rich business, and death business.

There must be something better."

Yes, there is. And it's inside of you.

It comes with every breath.

So I know that it is possible to know clearly without any uncertainty about your blessing every day; to understand, without doubt or question, the value of the breath, and to have come to a point where your gratitude is as sincere as possible for a human being. There's a lot of craziness in this world. But the hope for mankind is that there is something good in every single human being, too.

We have mastered the art of provoking the bad in people, but we have not learned the art of provoking the good in people. The consequences are murders, deaths, and wars. And people who have been in these wars have come home totally devastated.

CHANGE THE STRATEGY

The time for that beauty, that joy, to manifest is now, and it needs to begin with each person.

Peace is inside you, and you can feel it—not just know about it, but feel it every day.

Battles will come and go. We will win a few and lose a few. But the point is not the battles. The point is to win, and win, and win the war.

When you fight a war, you think you will win if you do this, this, and this, right? That's called *strategy*. What if you realize your strategy was wrong? Now don't try the same thing again. Change the strategy. You have looked outside; maybe it is time to look inside. You have believed in many things; maybe the time has come to know. You have made many excuses; maybe it is time to make the choice.

You can make the connection with the beauty inside. There's something very beautiful taking place in this life. You can be part of it.

Do you want to be happy, or do you want to be sad? Do you want to be fulfilled, or do you want to be empty? You have a choice.

Feeling peace, not once, but every day that I am alive, is winning the war.

It is possible to know clearly without any uncertainty about your blessing every day.

To understand,
without doubt or question,
the value of the breath,
and to have come to a point
where your gratitude is
as sincere as possible
for a human being.

TIME TO CHANGE THE STRATEGY

WE HAVE BEEN LOOKING EVERYWHERE EXCEPT WHERE IT IS.

When we discuss who we are, we say, "Man is the crown of the creation. The human being is intelligent, has language, and can do so many things. We have created technology. We have gone to the moon." So then one has to ask the obvious question: "If this is who we are, why are we in such a mess?"

Some say, "Man was created in the image of God." There seems to be a paradox. On one hand we have the possibility of peace, of joy, of knowing, of learning, of evolving, every single day. But that is not reflected in the situation of this world.

Are we not capable of exchanging bullets for caring and sharing? Of course we are. Then why do we choose bullets over caring and sharing? Are we not capable of creating? Then why do we choose destruction? Are we not capable of knowing? Then why do we choose ignorance? Are we not capable of being fulfilled? Then why do we choose emptiness?

THE WINDOW

I talk about peace, but it's not about the world. It's about the individuals, about every single human being. That's all that truly matters. You! You matter. The composition of existence is such that the ones that count are the ones that are living. There is a window, and in this window everything takes shape. The question is, how big is this window? One week, one month, one year, one lifetime? Or just a moment?

Are you set up for the moment? No! Absolutely not. We're set up for tomorrow, and the day after that. We're set up for five years from today. We're set up for ten years from today. We have the calendar system. And you can look at it and say, "There is January. And there is February. And there is March. And there is April," and so on and so forth. And where is the moment in this?

I talk about peace. But I don't go around explaining things to people. I don't say, "Oh, don't be confused about chapter eleven, line fourteen. Because this is what it really means." I don't have to explain. I merely have to present that which *is*—not that which is not, but that which is. I personally find that which *is* most fascinating, most interesting, most beautiful, most entertaining, most satisfying. My existence and your existence are not dependent on January, February, March, April, May, June. You cannot look at Death and say, "Well, the calendar isn't done yet. This is only July. It still goes on for August and September and so on. So come back later, December 31st." Wish it did, but it doesn't work that way.

THE LABELS

We say, "You are from this country, and I am from that country." People are born in Canada? Label: "Canadians." Defined by a line on a map—which does not exist, by the way. I have flown over it many times and couldn't find it. Birds don't seem to know about it. They don't come to the immigration office and say, "We are the geese coming in. This is our passport. Is it all right?"

Do mice know about it? Not a clue. Bees? Not a clue. Whales? Not a clue. I'm not being anti-patriotic. I'm just stating the obvious. We have labels for everything. There are the poor. Label: "Poor." And then there are the rich. Label: "Rich." And then there is "the middle class." You are defined not by being a human being, but by how much money you make.

What you know has no value. Your intelligence: no value. Who you really are: no value. The judgment is, "This is how much you make, so this is who you are."

SEVENTY PERCENT

So who are you, in reality? On one hand you are a shell that has been constructed brilliantly: bones, muscles, blood, guts, brain, and seventy percent water. Here is a neat trick: seventy percent water going to the moon. Seventy percent water saying "I am Doctor So-and-So." Seventy percent water saying "I am holy." Seventy percent water getting

dressed up and saying "Don't I look pretty?" And the other seventy percent water seeing that seventy percent water, and whistling!

So who are you? Seventy percent water? Or is there something else going on? The good news is, it's not the seventy percent water, it's how much consciousness you have that is going to make the difference in your existence. Consciousness! Even if it is one percent. Because that one percent is going to decide the fate of that seventy percent water—and everything else.

Seventy percent water getting dressed up and saying "Don't I look pretty?"

And the other seventy percent water whistling!

So who are you? You are, then, the most precious gift because you have the ability to know. You are, then, the most blessed, for you have been touched by the divine. Let me qualify. The divine I talk about is not a "he" or a "she". The divine was not born. The divine exists and will never die. Was, is, and will be. The divine favors all. No one label in particular. Everyone alive is touched by that divinity in a very special way, because it resides within all. You have the divine within you.

Don't get this confused with any religion. I'm talking about just you and the divine.

A REALITY

The divine that resides within you needs to be known, not believed in. Known. You can live your life surrounded by the beauty that is within you. This is who you are.

A reality, every single day. Not speculation, not an idea, not a thought. Not some imagination, but every single day honing the skill of being in touch with the beauty that resides inside you. That's when you become complete. That's when you become whole. That's when you can dance, you can understand, you can care, you can share, you can think, you can be conscious, you can be aware—not only for yourself, but for the ones around you.

A lot of people say to me, "You talk about peace. I don't see any peace inside of me." So I say to them, "From far away you see more, but you don't see the details. Come a little closer and you will see the detail!" I talk about the breath,

and people say, "What is in the breath? I mean, I breathe all the time." You don't see the detail? Come a little closer. To what? Not to me. Not to an idea, not to a theology, not to a philosophy, not to a system. Come closer to yourself, because this is where the magic is, this is where the miracle of breath is taking place.

Lots of people listen to me these days, since the downturn in the economy. At least they give me a few minutes of their time. Before that? "Ah, yeah, I don't have time for this stuff. I'm busy." Then an amazing thing happened. With all the seminars in the world about success, and all the people taking their success classes, and the successful being at the top of their game, everything collapsed. And people found that they were no longer successful.

In some countries the people who drove the economic downturn were the top-notch people, with the highest levels of education, specialists in their fields. They were taught everything except how not to be greedy. They were taught everything but to believe in the truth. So now people say, "Oh, peace! Maybe I have some use for it." But you don't have to be penniless to have peace. You can be the richest person and have peace; you can be the poorest person and have peace. There are no labels involved.

MIRACLES

So where is this peace? Let's see. If the divine is within you, it's a good bet that peace is within you, too. Where else would it be appropriate for the peace to be than in the heart of every single human being? To be understood, to be felt. That's how simple it is.

There are people who look for blessings. "Oh, please bless me. I need a miracle." What is your definition of a miracle? If you see milk coming out of a stone, that's not a miracle, that's an abnormal situation. What is a miracle? Seventy percent water that can hug. Seventy percent water that can say "I love you." Seventy percent water that can appreciate. Don't you think that's a miracle?

People say, "He walked on water! That's a miracle!" We all are seventy percent water, and we walk every day! Seventy percent water walking: is that not a miracle? I'm just stating the obvious.

And so if you look for the blessing of all blessings, there it is: You! The miracle of all miracles— there you are. You. Immeasurable joy—you. Companion to the divine—you. Alive—you. Existing in a moment—you. That's the obvious. Did you know that?

I know—I don't believe—I *know* that you know that. Now for every one of us the time has come to evolve, to understand that, and feel that, every day in our life. That's true evolving. That's true learning. That's true understanding. That's true knowing. Not some philosophy. Not some guilt. Not some vague understanding.

Some people say, "If the divine is within me, how come I don't know that?" Good question. You are so far away from yourself that you can't see yourself. Solution? Come closer to yourself and you will be amazed at what you can feel. There are answers that dance within you that don't even have questions.

Seventy percent water walking: is that not a miracle?

We are so enamored by questions. We think questions will lead us to answers. This has been going on for thousands and thousands of years. People have been chasing questions and not getting to the answers. Don't you think it's time to change the strategy? I think it's time to just start looking for answers. Even if you can't find the question, just find the answer.

CHANGE THE STRATEGY

We have tried the formula of war for thousands of years and it has not worked. Don't you think it's time to change the strategy? Try peace. It'll be cheaper. It won't cost trillions of dollars. And not only that. This is what most people on the face of this earth want. They want peace. They've had enough. Will somebody listen to them? I hope so.

The little babies, the little children, the mothers, the fathers, that's what they want. They want peace. And the time to change the strategy is here. If you don't feel blessed every day, then it is time to change the strategy. Because whatever you have been trying hasn't worked. In your life, you should have peace. You should have joy. You should have contentment. And if you don't, you have to change the strategy.

Where have you been looking for answers? Everywhere! You have been looking for answers every single place except for one. So, stating the obvious, that's the only place left. Change the strategy. Look within you, look within your heart, look within your understanding.

You think there is a shortage of food on the face of this earth? Do you know how much food is thrown away just in the garbage? This earth on which you live produces food in abundance. It's a giver! It takes care of you. You need to take care of it. That's humanity. Before we talk about all the things we're proud of: "Oh, we could go to the moon, and we could do this and that"—let's just be human. Even for a day, let's be human, just human and, in our humanity, search for the peace that lies within us.

Try peace. It won't cost trillions of dollars.

And it is what most people want.

They've had enough.

Will somebody listen to them?

Instead we are waiting. We're waiting for some angel to come out of the sky. We are waiting for the angel coming down with the wings! This beautiful, beautiful woman's face, and the flowing blond hair. And: "Okay, I am here, your savior." And how long have you been waiting for that? A few thousand years.

Time to change the strategy. Because the angel that you are waiting for has come. And you know who it is? It's you! Get on with the business of finding peace in yourself.

Where to look? I can help you with that. Minor point: it's within you. I'm not the one who's saying "You have to go up on top of that mountain." I don't even talk about tests, trials and tribulations. How can that be? Shouldn't we all be tested by the one that knows everything? But why would the one who knows everything want to test us? Don't they already know if we're going to pass or fail?

COME CLOSER

People say, "God works in mysterious ways." No, not a single mystery. The drop begins its journey from the ocean, becomes the cloud, goes to the mountains. Falls, becomes the river. Flows through the land and joins the ocean again. Mysterious? No. Been doing this for thousands and thousands of years, allowing civilizations to be formed on its banks. Distributing water. What a beautiful way to do it. So much for mysteries! As long as this breath is in you, you are alive. One day, this won't be, and you won't be. Is that mysterious? Absolutely not.

So come a little closer, and see the details. Come a little closer, and embrace the peace that lies within your heart. Because it is so beautiful.

Come closer to yourself and you will be amazed at what you can feel.

There are answers that dance within you that don't even have questions.

You can live your life
surrounded by the beauty
that is within you.

A reality, every single day.
Not speculation, not
an idea, not a thought.
Not some imagination,
but every single day
honing the skill of being in
touch with the beauty
that resides inside you.

That's when you become complete.
That's when you become whole.
That's when you can dance,
you can understand,
you can care, you can share,
you can think, you can be conscious,
you can be aware
—not only for yourself,
but for the ones
around you.

About Prem Rawat

Prem Rawat is a respected international speaker, attracting audiences from all walks of life. The honorary title "Ambassador of Peace" has been granted him by a number of governmental and academic institutions because of his ability to inspire audiences to see personal peace as a possibility for everyone.

As a speaker, Prem Rawat is both accessible and humorous, using stories, analogies, and even poetry to reach his diverse audience. At the same time he has an important message, that personal peace is a fundamental right for all.

He speaks from the heart, without script or rehearsal, bringing simplicity to important issues that people often find complex. His life's goal is to offer his message of peace to all seven billion of the world's population.

In pursuit of this goal, he maintains a challenging travel schedule, often flying over 100,000 nautical miles in a year. In 2012 alone he spoke to over 730,000 people at 102 live events worldwide. During that time, there were over a million downloads of his videos. He receives no recompense for his speaking engagements.

In addition to speaking in front of intimate audiences and vast crowds — sometimes exceeding 300,000 in India — he has been invited to speak at a number of important institutional venues and forums. These include the European Parliament, the United Nations (UN), the Italian Senate, the parliament buildings of Australia, Argentina and New Zealand, the Young Presidents' Organization, and the Guildhall in London, as well as numerous universities across the world.

RECENT ACHIEVEMENTS AND RECOGNITION

In November 2011, Prem was invited as keynote speaker and inspirer of the "Pledge to Peace" launched at the European Parliament, under the patronage of the First Vice-President, Gianni Pittella MEP. The Pledge to Peace, a call to peaceful action, was the first of its kind ever presented at the European Union, and which 37 institutions signed. The pledge activities, announced on UN Peace Day each year, continue to develop momentum.

In 2012, Prem was awarded the Asia Pacific Brands Association's BrandLaureate Lifetime Achievement award, reserved for statesmen and individuals whose actions and work have positively impacted the lives of people and the world at large. Other recipients of this prestigious award include Nelson Mandela and Hillary Clinton.

In the spring of 2012 he was invited to launch the Third Festival of Peace in Brazil. This initiative, hosted by UNIPAZ (University of International Peace), which works towards world peace, involved more than one million people.

Speaking in a specially prepared video for the Nordic Peace Conference in Oslo, Prem emphasized the very real possibility of peace in our lifetime. He said, "There are people who are very greedy, there are people who don't care. But in my opinion, that is a minority. The majority of the people on the face of this earth want peace, and if this is true, then peace on earth is a very achievable objective. People say it's not going to happen. Well, let this time belong to those who believe it can happen, not to the ones who say it cannot."

In recognition of his profound impact on individuals and his contribution towards the world's understanding of peace, Prem has received many keys to cities and awards, and has been named an Ambassador of Peace four times — by UNIPAZ and three other governmental organizations.

BACKGROUND

Born in December 1957 in rural India to a prominent family, Prem left his native land at age 13 to travel to Europe and America, with the desire to bring his message to the world. His driving ideal was to present to every person, an optimistic vision of life, a vision of peace, both individually and collectively. This ideal continues as strongly today, some four decades later.

HUMANITARIAN EFFORTS

In 2001, Prem Rawat created The Prem Rawat Foundation (TPRF), which addresses the fundamental human needs of food, water, and peace, so that people everywhere can live their lives with dignity, peace, and prosperity. In the 12 years since its inception, the Foundation has made 158 grants to assist people in need in 40 countries.

With TPRF's Peace Education Program, Prem has reached out to people in many walks of life. It has been particularly successful in prisons, helping those incarcerated to rehabilitate, experience hope, understanding, and self-worth. Prem has spoken at several of the 28 prisons where the program is currently running worldwide. The program is also now the subject of academic study due to its unusual success in reducing recidivism and in helping transform and give hope to those incarcerated.

PERSONAL

Prem Rawat embraces creativity and cutting-edge technology. He is an inventor, photographer and a highly accomplished pilot, with over 12,000 hours flying time, most of it spent flying himself to speaking engagements. He is married with four adult children and one grandchild.

Credits

PHOTOS

Mehau Kulyk:	1, 10-11, 12, 16-17, 21, 25, 36, 44, 55, 57, 63, 65, 71, 76, 77, 78, 80, 82, 84, 85, 87, 95, 110-111, 120, 122, 125, 135, 139, 142, 144-145, 154-55, 156
Peter Engberg:	26, 40, 48, 84, 106, 108, 130
Jens Brodersen:	59, 67, 90, 99
Jaques Masraff:	75 (top)
Gail Browne:	75 (bottom)
Wiki Commons:	52
iStock:	30, 33, 51, 101, 116, 149, 151

Mehau Kulyk is a photographer, living in London, UK

Peter Engberg is an award-winning filmmaker and photographer, living in Copenhagen, Denmark

Jens Brodersen is a tennis pro and photographer, living in Copenhagen, Denmark

ART DIRECTION	Jaro Mewes is a graphic designer and tutor of communication design, living in Hamburg, Germany
EDITOR	Ole Grünbaum is an award-winning author, journalist and newspaper editor, living in Copenhagen, Denmark
EDITORIAL ASSISTANCE	Pegi Hope Cohen, Lynne Laffie, Lorraine Chamberlain, Ron Geaves, Nicole Vanderhoop, Willow Baker, Rani Thoms

PREM RAWAT

THE GREATEST TRUTH OF ALL: YOU ARE ALIVE

Available in English, Spanish and German

Insightful and accessible, these discourses raise the important question of the relationship between peace in the world and peace in our internal lives . . .
Manuela Hoelterhoff, Winner Pulitzer Prize for Arts and Culture Critique

Within us there is a peace that does not depend on circumstances, a gift from existence itself . . . This is an important book that is quick to read but leaves a lasting feeling.
Carmen Posadas, Author, receiver of the Premio Planeta

This book can be read over and over and bring renewed understanding of what's most important to every human being.
Tim Gallwey, Author of the Inner Game books

Prem Rawat has found a way to decode the essence of "self-knowledge" and delivers it, to the reader, like a tall, cool drink of water on a hot summer day.
Mitch Ditkoff, Director, Idea Champions

A must for anyone who wishes to discover who they are. So simple. You are alive. But discover what life is.
Nick Koshnitsky, Customer review on Amazon

Prem Rawat has the rare quality of speaking directly to the heart of the reader. Simply and clearly he speaks of the essence that resides within all human beings . . . We are alive—there is no greater miracle than that.
Bill McCarthy, Customer review on Amazon

Made in the USA
San Bernardino, CA
28 January 2014